BULE GILA

BARTELE SANTEMA

BULE GILA

Tales of a Dutch Barman in Jakarta

EQUINOX
PUBLISHING
JAKARTA SINGAPORE

PT Equinox Publishing Indonesia
Menara Gracia 6/F
Jl. HR Rasuna Said Kav C-17
Jakarta 12940

www.EquinoxPublishing.com

ISBN 979-3780-04-5

Printed in Indonesia.

contents

introduction

I grew up feeding cows and riding horses on a farm in Friesland, the Netherlands. When I was fifteen years old I started my first business. I sold beer, french fries and burgers out of an old trailer. Every evening guys from the surrounding villages would drink my beer and listen to rock and roll on an old tape recorder. Big cities were considered our enemies. Deutz was voted the number one tractor.

Ten years later I decided I had finished with the farm life and relocated halfway around the world to Indonesia. I tried just about every job you can imagine: actor in a TV soap opera, cocoa quality controller (corruption from local partners forced the business to close), distributor of office equipment (the economic crisis of the late '90s caused my business to go belly-up) and interior contractor (with a bullying boss). By this time, I had had enough ups and downs, so I started dreaming again. I thought about the things that I really enjoyed: beer, women, rock and roll and, most importantly, not working for someone else. How could I combine all of these things into a viable business and have fun at the same time? After considering many ideas, the answer was so simple: I would open a bar.

I developed a business plan. The bar wouldn't be like other bars in Jakarta. It would be a friendly and open *Cheers*-type environment. Good-looking girls – lots of them – behind the bar, wearing whatever they wanted. It would be open every day and it would only close when the last person had left. And no staff would call any guest "mister". Ever!

With the support of several friends, I was *gila* enough to open a bar just after the economic crisis that made so many *bule* leave the country. The name BuGils, a combination of *bule* and *gila*, which loosely translates as "crazy white man" seemed appropriate. Bugil also means "naked" in Indonesian but that's another story. I found a perfect location: Taman Ria Senayan, where a vacant lot with a terrace facing onto the man-made lake was available.

Now, after five years in operation, BuGils Café is one of the most popular hangouts in Jakarta. In this place you still can find real characters, Indonesians and *bules* alike. It is damn difficult for many of these characters to stick to the established rules of behavior, ethics and principles. Good or bad, at least it gives me lots to write about.

The stories in this book are a compilation of experiences and observations I have witnessed and have written about in my weekly email newsletter over the past few years. And every single one is true. I see all too often foreigners criticizing Indonesia and its people, their habits and behavior and make fun of them or – even worse – get angry. Sure, I have my own weak moments from time to time, but in most of my stories I see us *bules* as victims of our own making: unwilling to adapt to our new surroundings.

I would like to thank Saddam Hussein for taking Iraqi airlines out of the skies in 1990, leaving me stranded on my first trip to Indonesia; my parents who didn't make me go back to the farm (although they keep trying); the staff for their loyalty and hard work over the years – while I was just sitting there dreaming and drinking; and Mark Hanusz for his long friendship and risking the reputation of his great publishing company by being associated with this book.

But my biggest thanks go to the BuGils regulars. Sometimes, at the end of a long night, we sit across from each other on both sides of the bar, going for the last round of tequila shots or B-52's. I shout at them, "Get a life you sad bunch of losers!" And they shout back, "Wanker! Alcoholic barman! Get a real job!" and then we cheers and have another round before the lights go out. Here's to many more drinks together, mates.

Bartele Santema
Jakarta, January 2005

"An intelligent man is sometimes forced
to be drunk
to spend time with fools."

Ernest Hemingway

bule gila

In support of the Dutch national team for the 1994 World Cup, I and some other Dutch guys from our FC Knudde football team had bright orange costumes made and we would all get together to watch the games of the Dutch football team.

For the first match, Elwin promised to pick me up from the Blora bus stop on Jalan Sudirman at three o'clock in the morning, in time to watch the game live on TV at four. I arrived at the bus stop and remember how strange it was to be the only person on Jakarta's main road. A busy, noisy and polluted road during the day, it was now dark and deserted, except for an occasional *kaki lima* passing by.

Then I heard the sweeping sound of a broom slowly coming towards me. I looked around and saw a road worker cleaning the street. He was wearing exactly the same orange outfit as me! The sweeper was still about fifty meters away when he stopped and looked up. Gazing for a second in my direction, he continued at a slightly increased speed. When he was about five meters away, he abruptly stopped, rested his chin on his broom and focused sharply on me. The man was in deep thought.

Then I heard another sweeper coming from the other side of Sudirman, not far from Hotel Indonesia. He dragged the broom lazily behind him as he approached us. This road worker had an orange shawl wrapped around his face, only his eyes were visible. It was a weird scene. The two sweepers were now standing next to each other. Both were speechless and were intensely staring at me. Finally, one of them asked me in a dry tone, "*Mau ke mana,* mister?" I realized the absurdity of the situation and answered: "I am going over to Jalan Rasuna Said. They told me that they need some help to clean the streets there. They're pretty dirty." At that point, Elwin in his old Feroza arrived at high speed. He was also wearing his orange outfit. I jumped in the car and we drove off, leaving two absolutely perplexed street cleaners behind.

Every time I come home late and see those orange-clad workers on Jalan Sudirman, I remember that scene and wonder what they must have been thinking. Why were two *bules* wearing street cleaner clothes on Jalan Sudirman at three in the morning? What was their conclusion? It probably had something to do with their final words as I jumped into Elwin's car: *bule gila.* It was the first time I heard those words, but it wouldn't be the last.

living with a gambler

Tony called himself a computer programmer. But three months after he had rented a room in my apartment, I discovered that in his whole life he had written just one program: a program to predict football scores. His previous five years in Hong Kong and Macau had ensured Tony a reputation in and around the casinos and horse tracks. He had managed to establish himself in a network of the world's big-time gamblers.

Tony didn't like to be called a bookmaker. He preferred "money-mover". He had no bad feelings about making a living from other people's losses. "Isn't that what insurance companies do? That's just gambling in another jacket," as he said last week when one his customers in London lost another 150,000 pounds.

In that first month in the apartment there wasn't much football to gamble on, so Tony played online Black Jack. Coming home from another night in BuGils, I would find Tony relaxed, sitting at his computer with a glass of his favorite wine while the piano played softly in the background. This scene would be intermittently interrupted by smooth seductive voices saying "Place your bets please" and once in a while a loud and excited "Black Jack! Player wins!" It must have been one of these nights that I came home after having a few too many beers that I decided to try out my own luck.

I registered myself under the name Lucky Bastard at the online Gold Club Casino. With an initial deposit of 100 bucks, I indeed became a Lucky Bastard. In half an hour I had earned $1200! The next evening I celebrated my gambling profits in BuGils and gave away more rounds in one night than I normally do in a month. Coming home, I stumbled into my apartment and was greeted by a conspiratorial voice: "Welcome to the Gold Club Casino, you Lucky Bastard!" Then with an upbeat invitation, the voice continued more loudly: "Place your bets please!" I couldn't resist and won again – this time the enormous sum of 2800 bucks. Lucky Bastard was on a roll! Tony tried to warn me but his well intended warnings were in vain. Sure enough, before the morning prayers had issued forth from the nearby mosque, no doubt condemning gambling and alcohol, all my not-so-hard-earned profits were gone.

The football season started. Tony was getting more and more nervous but soon had everything in place. There were four computers online 24 hours a day, and TVs showing all the soccer channels available. He even hired two full-time Chinese female employees, for as he explained to me: "Chinese can count and they can communicate in Cantonese with the bookmakers in Macau."

In the daytime he was busy arranging his credit cards, casino accounts, outstanding winnings, etc. At midday he started checking the prices at the different betting agents and bookmakers such as Ladbrokes, William Hill and Victor Chandler. More and more printouts filled the room. He would walk around in the growing chaos wearing nothing but his shorts.

When the moment of important decision-making arrived, he would dress himself up as if he was planning to go to church. His workday had started. International calls to Hong Kong, London and New York were made. Bets were carefully written down in a very small notebook he always carried with him. Then, just before the games would start, he would place his own bets. "I am going to put a fortune on Arsenal! They have gone totally nuts in Macau! The whole world is betting on Manchester! Manchester has to give away one goal to Arsenal! My program says it should be only half a goal!" By this stage Tony would have worked himself up into a state of ecstasy. The way he cried out his favorite bets for the night made me believe that I too should trust his predictions and also bet "a fortune".

I never heard Tony talking about players, only about statistics. "Emotional betting is deadly," he would say. When finally the bets were placed, it was "women time." Now if Tony had a few bad gambling nights, he would call in cheap Blok M girls, but during his winning streaks he would invite over his more respectable and rich Chinese girlfriends. After these interludes, later in the evening, the real show would begin. There would be Dutch football loud and live over the internet radio, goals scored in Germany announced by sharp, hair-raising whistles blasting out from the computer speakers, Italian and English football on the televisions, and Livescore.com for complete online updates.

At this stage Tony wouldn't speak a word, but would frantically move back and forth between the hardware. But every fifteen minutes he would lie down on his bed. This was an interesting behavior to analyze. Having his mattress on the floor, he would fall flat on it with his hands stretched alongside his body and his empty eyes staring wide open up at the ceiling. Then, after a few minutes, he would jump up again and swiftly move between the computers and television screens.

The staring fascinated me as did the sudden change from not wanting to miss anything to the fifteen minute breaks. What was going on in his head during those moments of empty staring? Why were his hands stretched straight alongside his long and skinny body? Was it some kind of re-charge position? Was he calculating the profits and losses, gauging his bets? I never found out.

After a full year of sharing an apartment with Tony, I am sure he had lost more than he had won. I am sure of it because I had never before – or since for that matter – seen so many ugly women coming in and out of my apartment.

Postscript: When the Indonesian government introduced new laws making it more difficult for foreigners to obtain residence visas, Tony decided to move to Macau permanently. He certainly is now making a profit. He has even bought an apartment there. His operation in Indonesia is still running and once in a while he comes to Jakarta to make sure everything is going smoothly. On the last occasion he came into BuGils, I pointed out the gorgeous Chinese girl at his side and asked him: "Could this be an emotional bet?" Tony looked at me for a second, started laughing, and repeated his credo: "You are right! It's just gambling in another jacket!"

the rain doctor

BuGils' second anniversary got off to a pleasant start with a nice afternoon sun filtering down through Jakarta's toxic haze. Sitting outside on the terrace by the stagnant reservoir with its rat-infested "floating" Italian restaurant, the first guests were enjoying the free-flowing beer. No one had any inkling of what was to happen later. That night, on January the 16th, torrential rains broke over Jakarta. This was the first BuGils event that was to be nearly drowned out by heavy rain.

Normally, to keep such events dry, we use the magical powers of Pak Arif, a senior cook at BuGils. He had kept us dry for two years. It is our way of guaranteeing clubs and organizations that any event held at BuGils will not be ruined by the rain as we have our own way of dealing with nature. We usually give Arif Rp50,000 to buy the materials he needs for his communication with the "other world". That is all he needs to buy the necessary items – salt, candles and yellow rice. He performs his "communications" in the middle of the night before the event. He cannot do his rituals without his small *keris* (traditional dagger). Without ever telling the BuGils shareholders, I had allowed him to count these late-night hours as overtime.

While the rain was still pouring down late that January evening, I came into the kitchen to check on how they were doing on such a busy night. Everything was fine, the kitchen staff said, but I noticed that Pak Arif was looking annoyed. He was not being his normal friendly self. "*Kenapa* (why), Pak Arif?" He nodded back at me but was clearly not up for a chat. Another member of the staff replied for him: "Pak Bart didn't ask Arif to keep the rain away!" I was astonished. I had indeed forgotten to ask him to perform his anti-rain magic. He was clearly disappointed. Pak Arif grumbled lowly about how he could have helped. I apologized. He didn't react but just continued to cut up the carrots.

Two weeks later it was still raining. I went to the kitchen. "Pak Arif, the rain still hasn't stopped. Can't you do something?" He replied sadly that he needed all of his power for his sick wife. He had married some months earlier and his newly wed was now six months pregnant. "She has a nerve disease and it has spread all over her body. She has a lot of pain and we are afraid that she will lose the baby. With my *keris* I can hypnotize her so that she doesn't feel the pain so much and can go to sleep." He looked exhausted. "I am sorry... I can't help at the moment," he said.

I called a Dutch doctor I knew and asked him for some advice about what to do with Arif's sick wife. It was indeed a very painful disease and one that was hard to treat and, because she was pregnant, antibiotics and painkillers could only be used in a limited way. The only thing I could do was to allow Arif to go home to be with his wife when the pain was at its worst. He seemed very relieved with this offer.

The rains finally began to subside. Actually, the weather had been improving ever since Arif had begun to spend more time with his wife. She felt better with Arif by her side. Then he whispered to me with a slight grin and explained that he had used some of his "spare power" to keep the rain away – this time free of charge.

One week later, a Dutch family with three children was sitting on the terrace. I greeted them in a friendly fashion. "Ho, ho! Bartele! One moment!" they called, "why does it take so long for your kitchen staff to prepare the simple snacks we ordered thirty minutes ago? " The mother was clearly annoyed. "I don't know," I replied, "I just arrived. Let me check." But I knew the reason already. Arif was not in the kitchen. He was nursing his wife. The night before I had noticed him in a trance executing strange movements with his *keris* behind the kitchen. He was moving the rain away. It was because of Pak Arif's "spare power" that this nice Dutch family could now sit outside in the sun, though obviously I could not explain that this was the reason why there was a problem with their order. They wanted their french fries and they wanted them quickly.

Postscript: Pak Arif's wife gave birth to a healthy daughter and the mother recovered fully in the end. Looking back on it, five years later, we have never had an event rained upon again.

However, Pak Arif's mystical powers later became questionable after he asked permission to dig a hole on our premises. He had had a dream that a holy *keris* was buried under the terrace. He had invited his master teacher from East Java to come and assist him in recovering the *keris* in a sacred ritual. For Pak Arif it would have meant attaining a higher level of mystical power. They smashed through the concrete and dug some exploratory holes in the terrace but didn't find anything. The guru went back to East Java and Pak Arif still refuses to speak about it. It must have been the most embarrassing moment of his entire *dukun* career.

ladyboys: should half-women pay half?

On several occasions in the past people have asked us for ganja as they thought it would naturally be available in an Amsterdam-style bar. But now the bar faced a new dilemma. A couple of *bancis* or ladyboys in tight pants were spotted in our premises. The bar manager, Widi, came to me in confusion. She asked if Linda and Rita should get free drinks as it was ladies night. It was not until then that I noticed them.

The bulges in their tight pants hinted at the potential nightmares (or fantasies perhaps) of many first time visitors to Asia. I looked at them and they both smiled in a friendly way from the other side of the bar before calling out in a deep, husky voice, "Hello muscles!" The customers around the bar couldn't help but start giggling, though remarkably none of them laughed out loud or made a remark. Perhaps they knew that a ladyboy's punch can be hard, though later events would prove otherwise.

Uci, the cashier, suggested that they pay half as they were "half-men, half-women." But Widi thought we should give them free drinks in order to avoid any problems and added with a smirk, "*dan mereka pakai toilet wanita kok*" (and they are already using the women's toilet). I agreed. Unfortunately they drank like men and stayed until closing.

The following night they came back. But already a number of regulars had started complaining that they didn't feel comfortable with two ladyboys seated next to them at the bar. When a regular would go to the toilet, a ladyboy would oftentimes follow to sneak a peak. If I didn't deal with it, it was clear that I would very quickly lose some of my regular customers. But how could I politely ask them to stay away from BuGils? However, Singga the waitress said she knew them and would have a quiet word with them.

As it happened I had just left BuGils when my Singaporean friend Paskaran called me. I told him that there was a girl named Linda waiting for him at the bar. Paskaran had to think for a second and then said that the only Linda he knew was his partner's secretary. "That might be the one!" I said and hung up.

The next morning I had two text messages on my handphone. The first one was from Singga: "Hi Bart, I told the ladyboys that some of the customers had complained about them and that you had asked me to speak to them. They said 'fuck you' so I don't think they will be coming back." Then I read the second SMS. It was from my friend Paskaran: "I came to BuGils last night and asked for Linda. It was not the Linda I had hoped for. The customers looked at me as if I was some kind of weirdo thinking that Linda was my date! And for some reason all your staff now call me 'muscles'. You bastard!"

Postscript: One of the ladyboys came back a few times with a 'normal' female friend and her *bule* boyfriend. This new girl constantly teased and complained and upset my staff. Every time this threesome would visit BuGils, the staff would send one of the new girls to serve them. When Rini was still new, the 'normal' girl, either drunk or just looking for a fight, accused Rini of touching her boyfriend and warned her to stop. The other staff members watched the exchange from a distance. Rini vehemently denied that she had touched the girl's boyfriend. Then the girl pushed Rini. Drinks fell to the ground. Rini pushed the girl back. Then the ladyboy started to push Rini as well and a fight broke out.

Before I could interfere, all the female staff had jumped into the fray to help Rini. In a yelling, scuffling maul of girls, the ladyboy and her friend were thrown out of BuGils. The BuGils girls then chased the couple across the parking lot, up the crumbling cement stairs and out of the Taman Ria complex, with the apologizing boyfriend running after.

BuGils erupted with applause when they returned.

on shaky ground

Just as I was looking over a new plans for an outside bar in front of BuGils, the Taman Ria Senayan management called me. They informed me that they were planning to extend their parking lot to the area in front of BuGils in order to open up enough space for another forty-five cars. Previously they had said BuGils was not allowed to organize events there because the foundations were not strong enough! Apparently there was an enormous waste cache below the paving. But Taman Ria management didn't see the weight of all those cars as a problem. As they explained to me: "There is indeed a risk, Mr. Bartele, but this area will only be for valet parking – so if something happens, the number of casualties will be minimal." Answers like that didn't surprise me anymore.

Last month they politely asked me to remove my 1974 Holden that I had left out for sale in the parking lot. "It's because we have to ensure the view, Mr. Bart. That old car is a disgrace to the environment!" Being the good tenant that I am, I promptly removed my car and then called the property manager. I asked him, now that the one eyesore had been removed, would it be possible to kindly remove the dilapidated sinking ship in front of BuGils. The ship used to be an Italian restaurant but had completely fallen apart after it had been closed down a year earlier.

I explained to him, as management had explained to me, that the ship disturbed the lovely panoramic view of the lake. He laughed loudly. "Sure!" he answered. "If Mister Bartele's kitchen staff can help push the boat away, please go ahead! Ha, ha!" I wasn't pleased. Feeling a bit spiteful, I replied angrily: "Is this because you have virtually no staff left? Are your workers still in jail for last month's robberies at BuGils?' He stopped laughing, was quiet for a second, and then promptly hung up. My secretary gave me a concerned look: "You can't talk to them like that! They won't respect you anymore!" I couldn't have cared less and ended the issue: "If the valet boys go down, I hope he goes down with them…."

Postscript: As one might have suspected, the plans for the parking lot never got past the drawing board. Two years later, the ship, a huge rotting wood and concrete skeleton, a perfect hideout for rats, continues to disintegrate and "ensure" the panoramic view. And regarding my reference to Taman Ria workers in jail, a number of break-ins at BuGils kept us busy for weeks. Initially the general manager did not want to investigate the matter and refused to dispatch more security as he assumed it probably was my own staff who were the culprits. The matter was finally resolved when some Taman Ria maintenance workers were caught trying to get away with our TV. The general manager of course tried to save face. "We already suspected them," he explained. "We were just trying to trick them by pretending that we suspected the BuGils staff."

Whatever. To get the TV back I had to negotiate with the local police commander. The TV was on his desk and next to the commander was some guy chained to his chair. Obviously a criminal, he was polishing the commander's shoes. For Rp500,000 I got the TV back and I am sure that for another Rp100,000 I could have also unchained the shoe polisher to carry the TV to my car. Unfortunately I was out of cash.

plastic

My mother called me and told me to buy some plants. She had probably read something about the pollution in Jakarta as well as the bomb threats and decided to kill two birds with one stone. Her solution to my worries was to buy plants and put them in front of BuGils. It will not only create a healthier environment but will provide camouflage from the bombers. Being the good son that I am, I ordered my staff to buy some plants. When they came back, I found that they had bought plastic ones! Why not real ones? Because these plastic trees came with a special offer: free plastic birds! I complimented them with the fantastic deal they had made.

This morning I called my mother and told her I had followed her advice. I didn't tell her the plants were plastic, but I told her we now have little birds in the bar. "Birds in the bar are not good, son. They can carry diseases. SARS hasn't been solved yet. You better get rid of them!" In the background I could hear my father entering the house with his two dogs. They were barking loudly. "Is that Bart? Tell him to be more careful with these things he writes on the internet. Terrorists are everywhere. I'll ship him one of these dogs to protect him!" While my mother tried to calm down the dogs, my father picked up the telephone. I told him Indonesians don't like dogs and it might frighten customers away. "My son, that is because they have never seen a real dog! These Dobermans are from a German breed. They are reliable, good characters!"

Although I was always taught to listen and follow one's parents' advice, I am not so sure anymore. Maybe it is because they are getting older, maybe it is because things work differently at this end of the world. I think I actually like the birds. Silent plastic birds in odorless plastic trees. It was a good deal. I think I shall keep them in the bar as a kind of silent protest. It is my little private protest against deforestation and also against the pollution. Now let's see where I can buy some plastic dogs. I don't need pedigree papers. At this end of the world they are probably fake anyway.

Postscript: Indonesians like plastic flowers. Every house has them. Like the chairs and the mattresses that they buy, they normally keep them wrapped in plastic packaging as long as possible. The latest trees on Jalan Sudirman are nowadays made of plastic. The trees I bought at that time are still in BuGils but the plastic birds have already gone. They have been stolen by unreliable characters. So it seems I really do need a real dog in the end.

three floors and counting

Every year on her birthday I ask Widi the same question. This year her answer made me realize that all my drinking, and all your drinking, and thus the whole business is worth it. I recruited Widi from a restaurant where she used to sweep the floors. BuGils had been in operation for five months when I hired her. She has always been one my most loyal employees. When I asked her for the first time what she did with all the money she earned in BuGils, she proudly told me that she had started renovating her parents' house. It would soon be a complete concrete house. That was three years ago. The following year I asked her again and Widi, even more proudly, told me that they were now making a second floor on the house. She did complain however that the contractors never seem to finish the job. I recalled that the few times I had called her at home, I always heard the hammering of carpenters and plumbers in the background.

Last year, on her birthday, I asked Widi again what she does with the money she earns. While pouring a beer, she looked at me for a second. She scraped off the foam and her few seconds of silence indicated that it was an important question for her and that she needed a clear answer. She left the beer and came around from behind the bar and sat down next to me. "These contractors, Bart.

They take all the money. Already for three years!" "What! Your parent's house isn't finished yet?" "I thought they were already finished last year with that second floor!" Very slowly she turned her head to me and looked at me with sad and tired eyes: "Third floor, Bart. It's that damn third floor. They never seem to finish it."

Postscript: I don't know if I can keep Widi for another year, but if she stays it wouldn't surprise me if that same contractor is going to build the tallest house in Java. My beer that night tasted better than ever. I am comforted with the fact that our drinking is not for nothing. While writing this I feel the urge to call Widi's house – just to listen to the music of the hammers on that third floor.

what was she doing there?

I was enjoying a hot coffee in Starbucks when I when I received a panicked call from my staff. Uniformed government officials were "all over the place!" Apparently we were not supposed to sell alcohol one day before Ramadhan. I had always been proud that in BuGils' history we have never been closed. I could smell trouble. I quickly finished my lunch and headed back to BuGils. On the way the staff called three times asking nervously if I was almost there yet. In the parking lot, I saw five or six uniformed city officials sitting on the side of the street and smoking kretek. Two others were fast asleep in the back of a small, open truck. On the BuGils' terrace another three of them were lounging in the chairs.

Inside there were yet another two officials – the leader and his assistant. They were busily finalizing some kind of warning letter. I found out that when these guys first walked into BuGils they had asked if we were selling alcohol. "Of course!" my waitress happily informed them. "Please sit down and I'll bring you the menu. Or do you just want a draft beer?"

The leader presented me a letter that stated that BuGils was not obeying the rules as we had 'open' bottles of alcohol displayed. He pointed to the gin and whisky bottles behind the bar and then informed me that I had to come to his office on Monday morning at ten o'clock. Only there, in his office with his superior, could we discuss how much I would have to pay them for this offence.

So that Monday morning I went along to their office. The guy behind the desk started off by bullying me, but I had met too many of them over the years and I wasn't shaken by it. If it really was such a big mistake, I calmly told him, then my director would take care of it. Now he became a bit more careful. "Who is your director?" he asked. "A general," I answered. I don't like to use this tactic, but it was Monday morning and I was not planning to spend one minute longer there than I had to. His attitude changed. He suddenly became friendly.

Then I noticed this girl wearing a green government uniform in the back of the office, typing on an old computer. She was beautiful. I must have been staring at her for a while because the official opposite me suddenly bowed forward: "What is your religion?" "Crislam," I answered. He started laughing. I was funny, he concluded. The girl looked up and threw a short, shy smile at me. She would fit in the BuGils team well, I thought. Back to business.

The official told me that he was not able to inform me on the exact consequences of having bottles on display. I would have to wait for his superior. I had no idea how many superiors I would eventually have to meet so I decided to leave but not before the man had explained to me once more that he was only following the rules, that he was Christian, and that all decisions were up to his superior. I just had to wait for orders from above.

lifestyle concerns

My mother was not happy with the BuGils calendar I had sent her – twelve months of sexy girls with naughty looks. After she looked at the calendar she was convinced that I was in some kind of dodgy business. I forgot that it is a different world in which I am living here and that mindsets are different. Although the pictures on the calendar didn't show that much nudity, my mother did not want the calendar in the house. My father, on the other hand, suggested hanging it in the milking area as a kind of project to see if it would stimulate his cows to make more milk.

I explained to him that the girls in the pictures were actually working for me in the bar. He didn't believe me. "Yeah, sure son," he said. "When are you coming back anyway? There is a lot of work to be done here on the farm. And bring some of your staff with you, especially the January girl. She looks like she can do some hard labor. And the September girl can help your mother in the kitchen." I asked him what he thought of the December girl. "Oh, the half-naked one with the bottle of Bintang in front of her? Bring that one for your brother!"

He was clearly enjoying his plan. "It sounds like dad wants to set up in the illegal women trafficking business!" I said jokingly. "Mom will not be happy with that! Ha, ha!" At that point my mother took back the telephone and repeated her concerns over my lifestyle in Jakarta. It had become a routine thing. I explained to her that I was running a respectable business and that even ambassadors and ministers were visiting my place. I heard my father in the background calling out his last remarks just before disappearing again to work with his horses and cows: "Leave him mother! He is doing all right! After all, he hasn't asked us to send money for the last five years, has he?'

My father was happy with the calendar. I am absolutely sure of it.

Postscript: The 2004 BuGils calendar was widely considered a success and we had orders from all around the world. The staff would sign messages across their bared legs. They felt like real models. My mother finally realized that I was indeed running a respectable place when in the first months of the operation a Dutch minister came to Jakarta. I was informed by the Dutch embassy that Minister Jorritsma was planning to come to BuGils and that I should prepare a karaoke system.

The news that Jorritsma would visit BuGils spread quickly around Dutch society in Jakarta. The whole day I received phone calls from people asking me what time she would come. Knowing that this group never spent much anyway and that they only wanted to come to meet this VIP, I told them that she would come at seven o'clock in the evening. From the information provided by the embassy I already knew that in fact she would not arrive before nearly midnight.

The Dutch elite came in large numbers and much too early. No one ordered more then a cup of tea. After one hour of waiting they started asking questions. I kept on saying that she could come at any moment. The elite kept waiting. But hour after hour passed and there was no sign of the minister. Many of them left disappointed. But finally, around midnight, she came and stayed until 3:30 in the morning.

One embassy staff member, who accompanied her that night, came to me and said. "It's really strange that there are not more Dutch people here, many of them wanted to meet her. I told them that they should come here." "Yeah," I replied dryly, "that *is* strange. Really strange…."

my regulars care

I must say that so far I have been lucky in BuGils. We have never had a fight in the whole five years that we have been open. Well, that's not quite true. I remember one Irishman who knocked over some tables and chairs. But I don't count that one. After all, the man was Irish and drunk – how come these words go together so well? – for them it's a cultural thing.

Late last night there was a close encounter though. One guest was talking politely to a woman at the bar, not knowing that she had a boyfriend playing pool nearby. Suddenly the pool player started gesticulating with his stick to make it clear that it was his girlfriend that the man at the bar was talking to. The man at the bar was not happy with the pool player's rude behavior and got up. I knew both men and I knew they were both nice guys, not people you would expect to start a fight. So I wrestled myself in between them and tried to calm them down. They kept on arguing and created a tense atmosphere. One said he hadn't known it was the other's girlfriend, the other said he saw him putting his hand around her. It started to escalate until I whispered something in the larger one's ear. My arms were still clinched around his body to prevent him from attacking the other guy.

He suddenly stopped, looked at me and said: "You

mean … more then me?" "Yes," I told him. The man looked at me, smiled and said: "OK then, in that case I am sorry." Both men shook hands and the apologies went back and forth. Peace returned to BuGils, that friendly, cozy bar with the terrace in front of the clear blue waters of the Taman Ria lake filled with swans.

I was already on the way home when one of the regulars called me. He said: "How did you calm that big man down so suddenly? What did you whisper in his ear?" I laughed and said: "I told him that he could fight with anybody he wanted, but not with my best customer. Nobody spent as much as that man in BuGils and I could not afford to lose him, so I told him to back off!" I am lucky to have regulars like mine – they care.

papa stupid

This German was sitting at the bar chatting with a man who left later that evening without paying. The staff tried to collect the unpaid bill from the German who was enjoying another beer. He became upset and, of course, refused to pay. "But you know him! He's your friend!" the waitress countered. "No!" the German yelled back, hitting his fist on the bar. "I just met him!" He asked for the manager.

The problem was corrected and I offered the German a free beer. He turned out to be very friendly, and gave me some interesting things to think about. For example, he thought that in Indonesia, when a child bumps her head on a door, the child is taught to kick the door. If they trip over a shoe, they are encouraged to throw the shoe at the wall. The point he was making is it is always the fault of the object, never the person. It made sense to me. In the case of the guy who left without paying, my staff failed to collect money from a customer, so they tried to correct their mistake by blaming an innocent third person.

In that same week I saw my daughter Patricia, eighteen months old, hit her head by mistake on the dining room table and start crying. The babysitter then told her to hit the table and seconds later she was slamming both her little fists on it. I stopped her and tried to make it clear that it was not the table's fault, but hers. So, as an example, I hit myself: "Bam Bam! Papa stupid!" She stopped crying and stared at me with her big eyes. The babysitter looked puzzled as well and then slowly moved the table a bit further away from us. I thought they understood.

A day later Patricia was playing in front of the TV. When I came in she jumped up, and in her enthusiasm, banged her head against the kitchen door. She began to cry instantly while rubbing her head. Then she stopped, looked angrily at the door and lifted her hand, ready to attack it. I scolded her: "Hey, Patricia! What did I teach you? It's not the door's fault!" She turned towards me. When I bent down to pick her up, her hand came down hard on my head: "Bam Bam! Papa stupid!"

Postscript: Once a year I always do a staff review. In separate interviews the staff members are evaluated and their performance is discussed. One sure outcome of the discussions is that the individual female staff members always complain about the discipline of the rest of the female staff. Without exception! I always wondered if it was a means of self-defense or just a way to avoid taking responsibility for their own mistakes.

The most incredible example of this that I recall was a girlfriend I once had. She once asked if she could borrow my car to "*pulang kampung*" and said that her nephew would drive. A few days after they left, I received a call from Yogyakarta, explaining that they had totaled the car. They were injured but luckily not seriously. Unbelievably, my girlfriend was absolutely furious at me! It was entirely my fault she shouted! I couldn't believe it! Why? Apparently the reason that they had skidded off the road was because the tires were bald and that this was because I always went to Blok M to get drunk and then drove home so fast that I had no treads left on the tires. Shortly afterwards I found out that the driver wasn't her nephew but her "spare" boyfriend. Bam Bam! Papa stupid!

having my period

"Do you already have free wi-fi service in Starbucks?" "Yes, we do!" the lady behind the counter answered happily. I ordered my coffee, opened my laptop and got ready to write a new story. At that moment one of the staff came over to me to apologize that the free internet service didn't work yet. I fell back in my chair disappointed as last week exactly the same thing had happened to me in Plaza Indonesia and a day later in Cilandak Town Square.

A nice looking girl, sitting on a sofa opposite me, threw me a small grin with sleepy eyes. She was well dressed, was reading a *Vogue* magazine, and probably had never heard of Lintas Melawai or Blok M for that matter. I took a sip of my coffee and looked at her again. Our eyes met for a second and it made me a bit nervous. My next sip was too hasty and I had to wipe the cream off my nose. The girl lifted her magazine to cover her face, obviously hiding her laughter. Forget it, I thought – she is too beautiful and high-class for a Frisian farmer's son/bar manager/illegal Belgian beer dealer!

So I decided to do some work on my laptop and tried not to look up too often. I could feel she was looking at me and when I left half an hour later, I asked the waitress to give my name card to her. It was not really very courageous of me, but maybe she was waiting for some guy that would show up at any moment. Shortly after I left, I received a text message: "Hi hi hi! I was just planning to give you my name card! My name is Chacha. Call me!" Wow! She was to the point! I called her. She was walking to her car. A girl with a car? Would it be my lucky day? She was on the way to a film shoot but she was prepared to meet me in BuGils that night. Was she rich and famous? It was all too good to be true.

That night BuGils was packed. It was ladies' night and the house was rocking. Within the space of one hour Chacha sent me four messages to tell me that she was on her way. I became impatient. I decided to call her. She insisted over the phone that she would be there in ten minutes. I waited for another half an hour.

Then an SMS came through with an excuse that I hadn't heard before in all my years in Indonesia: "My dear Bart, I am so sorry I can't meet you now coz I got my period. Sorry iya." In the last ten minutes, on her way to BuGils, she had suddenly had her period!

In the past we had to stop some ladyboys from coming into BuGils, but I would never stop women having their period! Disappointed I leaned back in my chair. I looked to my left from where this lady next to the jukebox threw me a flirting smile. Oh no! It was the ladyboy again. When will *you* have *your* period and stay home!

Postscript: I did manage to meet the girl again and took her out to dinner. She was definitely a knock out and it was a pleasant evening. But I could feel something was not right. I don't trust people with two handphones and my suspicions were soon justified. A few days later she called me and asked for money for her sick brother who was in the Cikini hospital. He had had an accident. He had to be operated on urgently and she didn't have the money. What about her parents? Both were dead already. Couldn't she sell one of her handphones? She had lost one. Then she became angry and turned into a completely different person from the one I had met a few days earlier. "You don't trust me? If he dies it is your fault!" I asked her for the room number and her brother's name so I could bring the money over myself. With a "fuck you" she hung up the phone.

Two weeks later I saw her again in Starbucks, but this time from a distance. She was sitting with another *bule*, who was listening intently to her stories. I am sure the poor guy was new in town but I didn't bother to warn him. If you ever meet a girl with two handphones and a dying brother, you'd better be careful.

govvelldomme!

This middle-aged Dutch guy I know decided to get his front teeth fixed. He spent one month going in and out of the dentist's office and for five million rupiah, he got a set of dentures to replace his crooked teeth. He decided to come to BuGils and proudly show the regulars and staff his new smile. After a couple of beers he accepted a challenge to play a game of pool with another regular.

Meanwhile, I was chatting with the cashier next to the pool table when I heard a small thunk, followed by hollow rattling sound behind me. After a moment of silence, I heard someone shout "GOVVELLDOMME!" I turned around and saw the panicked face and bulging eyes of the Dutchman hanging over the pool table. He had his hand stuck deep in a corner pocket. "My teef! My damn teef fell flu fle flocket!" He then stuck his other arm in the pocket but to no avail. He tried desperately from all angles. By this time a crowd of spectators had gathered around the table and were laughing hysterically while the Dutchman, deadly serious, was ramming his entire arm into the corner pocket.

"I paid five million flor fhis fling! I just got it flis florning! It's flucking flidiculous!" he was yelling. Coolly, I suggested, "Why don't you try to roll a few balls through the pockets?" He freaked out even more. "Nooooo! You'll ruin my teef!"

We tried to lift the upper part of the pool table but it was too heavy. The kitchen staff tried to fish it out with forks but it was no use. After half an hour we gave up and decided to try again the next day. There would be no pool that night. Defeated by the pool table, the Dutchman settled himself at the bar. Some women quietly moved a bit further away from him. I was not sure if it was the scary toothless look he had or the way he spat while he tried to tell his story.

The next morning I got a call from one of the kitchen guys. "Mr. Bart, we finally managed to get the top off the table and we found his teeth, but did he really pay five million rupiah for this?" The kitchen guy continued: "Mr. Bart, golden teeth *di mana*? For five million rupiah I would expect gold teeth! I have a brother who can make teeth for half that price!"

why my babysitter wears a uniform

For years I hated to see the rich families strolling through malls with their little *kampung* babysitter in a light blue or white uniform, trying to control the spoiled kids. Even more terrible are the surgical masks they have to wear – as if they have some kind of incurable disease. I have always been against degrading maids and babysitters by making them wear silly things, but not anymore. I now insist that my babysitter wears a uniform.

Let me explain. I went to Pelabuhan Ratu together with my year-old daughter and her fifty-year-old babysitter. This old nanny did not wear a uniform. I had a relaxed weekend in the Padi Padi Hotel but noticed that after a day or so there the staff kept looking at us strangely. Especially at me. It didn't bother me, although I found it difficult to joke with the local staff as they kept their distance. More than once I saw them whispering and looking at us with an almost disgusted expression on their faces. The babysitter was more talkative then ever and clearly enjoyed the weekend away from the city.

A month later, I went back to the same hotel with some friends but left Patricia and the old *ibu* at home. "Aren't your daughter and wife coming?" the reception staff asked me hesitantly. I was shocked and answered, "What!? My wife? I don't have a wife. I am single. I am a single parent!"

The staff looked completely confused. "But the *ibu* said she was your wife!" It suddenly became clear to me. The old lady presented herself as my lovely wife on our second honeymoon!

When I came home a day later the *ibu* was sitting on the couch, feet on the table. My computer was on, a card game on the screen. The telephone was on her left, and a bowl of Indomie on her right. Complete anarchy! I gave her two months salary and told her to leave.

I now have a new babysitter from an agency with a "no good, money back" guarantee. She is quiet, young and most importantly, wears this nice light blue uniform. A few days after I hired her we all went shopping in the mall. Queuing for the cashier I overheard two middle-aged women behind me talking to each other, not knowing that I speak Bahasa Indonesia: "You think she's the *bule's* wife?" "Noooo…" said the other. "Too *kampung* for him." "But *bules* like *kampung* women," the other declared. "Yes, mmmm…maybe you are right, but the child is so pretty and well dressed." I didn't say anything and it was not until that moment that I noticed that my babysitter wasn't wearing her uniform! Not again! It turned out that she only had one, and that one was being washed. I immediately gave her money to buy two more.

If one day this nanny also starts pretending that she is my wife, I will insist that she wears one of those nice white surgical masks. That will teach surely teach her….

Postscript: I tried to explain the above to my father, but he always connects it with his animals back on the farm. He thinks that I have been here for too long. Face masks are for sheep with coughing disease. I should come back. "Why are you going on a holiday with a fifty year old? Your babysitter? That country is full with women. Find a wife." I gave up trying to explain things to my parents. Maybe I should go back. But how to find a babysitter in Holland that has a "no good, money back" guarantee?

birman

One of my earliest and best friends in Indonesia is also the dirtiest, smelliest and most extraordinary character I've met in Jakarta so far. His name is Birman. His job is selling newspapers. His clothes are blackened with dirt, as are his hands and face. If you dive deep into an Indonesian garbage pile, you will smell Birman. You might even find him in there. But he earns more money than an ordinary office worker.

His motorbike is fast. It has to be fast because a few times a week he has to pick up the newspapers from the airport before anybody else gets them. He buys the second-hand newspapers from the cleaners of KLM or Garuda planes and then speeds back to Jalan Jaksa, to BuGils or to one of his many other customers. He even irons the papers so that they look new again. I tried to convince him to make himself look better as he still hopes to find a wife one day. But Birman prefers to stay dirty as he thinks women will only want his money once he looks and smells good. When I gave him some of my old clothes, he was very thankful, and as a way of expressing his appreciation he even managed to get a group of German tourists from Jalan Jaksa to come to my bar!

From that time on I instructed the staff to give Birman the honor of a tall glass of beer every time he comes to the bar – but only one though as the smell is unbearable. Wherever he sits down with his glass of beer, a vacuum forms with a radius of two meters around him. All the clothes I gave him he sold and nowadays a lot of the hoodlums on the streets of Jalan Jaksa can be seen wearing "Friesland Boppe" T-shirts.

The only clean thing on him is the stack of newspapers sticking out of his backpack. Birman stutters but is not stupid. He knows when to sell his newspapers, that is, after people have had a few beers. And he always tries to sell the oldest newspapers first. If the customers aren't interested in his selection, he leaves and comes back half an hour later with the latest editions. Usually people forget to take the newspapers back home so, after the customers leave, Birman comes back and picks up the papers that have been left behind at the bar.

One day this American oil tycoon was a bit annoyed when Birman offered his Dutch newspapers to him. "Newspapers? I'll buy all your fucking newspapers!" the American shouted. He slammed a $100 note on the bar. Birman's eyes started flashing. His movements became uncontrollable. He scuffled back and forth. He stuttered a few words and finally dropped all the papers on the ground. He grabbed the money from the bar and ran out the door. The American didn't even look at the newspapers or at Birman but continued his conversation with his partners. Later that night Birman came back and slyly collected up all the papers. He had had a good day.

I will be happy to introduce you to Birman next time he comes to BuGils. You will easily recognize him. You will smell him. He's my best friend, good old Birman. Characters like him make life colorful. Oh, by the way, ladies – he is still single. I'll have him deliver newspapers to your house so you can get to know him better.

Postscript: These days Birman comes less often to BuGils, mainly because he now has a home delivery service. One Dutch businessman recalled that while he was in an important meeting, Birman suddenly walked into the meeting room. Somehow he had gotten past security and reception and came scuffling in through the door. He wanted to deliver the newspaper personally as he was not sure it was the right address. He was virtually black with dirt, he was filthy and he smelled terrible. The result was total astonishment in the meeting room.

Another time I noticed a mean-looking security guard in front of the legendary Tanamur discotheque. He was wearing a BuGils T-shirt. Enthusiastically I gave him a thumbs up sign. The guy came towards me and asked me if I wanted to buy shirts like the one he was wearing. "Do you sell them?" I asked in surprise. "No. A guy called Birman does. He can supply you with them very cheaply!" Birman had obviously managed to help himself to some shirts from our warehouse!

The last time that I saw Birman was in Yogyakarta while we were on an outing. Sitting in a restaurant I suddenly noticed Birman come scuffling in with his newspapers. When he noticed me he started hyperventilating. The restaurant manager wanted to chase him out, but I offered him a chair. He told me that when he finishes his deliveries in Jakarta, he brings the unsold papers with him on a freight train to Yogya every weekend! He then sells them to tourists and then rides the thousand kilometers back again on Sunday night. I congratulated him on being the hardest-working person I know and he just flashed a wide yellow-toothed grin at me: "No…no…no…not only that," he stammered. "Th…th…the girls are cheaper here too!"

sex gymnastics

It happened on the dock of a Pulau Seribu island. We were on another staff outing and had just finished a great dinner on the jetty under the star-lit sky. Some of the staff went back to their huts, some remained to play pool, and others lounged around on sofas listening to Iwan Fals' music. I was dreaming away, looking over the dark sea and enjoying the peaceful night. Small waves calmly lapped against the rocks on the shore in front of me.

Then, on the dock, I noticed our cashier Uci lying on her back. Endjie was lying next to her, hands on her hips, pushing her behind up in the air. For a second I thought something had happened as they were both making strange movements with their hips. The movements were slow and sometimes fast. Their bodies swung up and down and from left to right. I quickly took a few gulps from my bottle of Bintang. It was dark and I didn't want to be a dirty sneaker so I politely coughed a few times.

"Oh, hi Bart! Uci is showing me what she learns at her school!" Endjie reacted enthusiastically, still keeping her position with her hands on her side and pelvis thrust into the sky. I couldn't believe it! "What? School? What school?" I asked in disbelief. Uci slowly got up while pulling her tight shirt down and explained: "Sex gymnastics. This course is something new in Indonesia. They teach you to train certain muscles." She was looking so serious, it had to be true. "Is there a school for that?" "Yes. On Jalan Radio Dalam. The teacher is from Madura, just like me."

Some readers will think that I must be the happiest man with the best job in the world. Others will think I am a pervert whose main pleasure is hiring sexy girls for a bar. I consider myself to be a happy observer only. While the two staff members continued their practice that night on Pulau Macan, I went to the other end of the island with a six-pack of beer. I stayed there until I was sure they had finished their training.

Madura is an island famous for bull races and for the powers the women have to satisfy their husbands. Ask any Indonesian about the story of Madurese women and they will break out into their biggest smiles. Is it true that they have special powers? The rumors are that they are trained by their grandmothers. They lift heavy weights with their feet from the age of ten and they learn how to make special jamu or herbal drinks. Is it true? This week I asked Uci if it was OK with her to interview her about the Madura myth. "Sure," she said. "What do you want to know? The jamu part or the technical part?" She gave me that same look as she gave me a year earlier on the jetty at that staff outing.

I closed my laptop, ordered the heaviest Belgian beer BuGils had to offer and went outside to sit down on the terrace. The green water of Taman Ria Lake was still. The sky was grey with smoke. It is not an easy job. It is a damn difficult job running a bar in Jakarta.

the toolbox from perth

I met Wendy a year earlier in a supermarket and went out with her that same evening. We met for dinner at Koi, a restaurant popular with the expat crowd. Wendy, originally from Jakarta, had been living in Perth with her Australian husband for two years and she recently moved back to Indonesia. She explained she had divorced two months earlier. When I asked why, she just shook her head and said, "He was always so jealous." During the first glass of wine she told she had worked in a restaurant. After another glass, it was a bar and, and hour later when the bottle was almost finished, she confessed it was actually a strip club and she was an erotic dancer.

She made 4,000 dollars a month dancing naked on the bar, but because her visa expired she had to return to Jakarta. She was clearly disappointed. At that point two good-looking ladies sat down at a table next to us. With sleepy but sparkling eyes Wendy began staring at one of the two women. I snapped my fingers to get her back to our conversation. I ordered another bottle of wine. She said, "I'll tell you a secret." She bent forward over the table towards me and continued in a whisper, "I am actually bisexual." Then she leaned back again and with a big smile, hands crossed over her breasts, waited for my reaction.

I was indeed a little shocked and was wondering what

other surprises were in store for me. "So, in Perth, for your work, you also were involved in…uhhh…uhhh…" I stammered. She enthusiastically responded: "Oh, man! The parties I was involved in – you wouldn't believe it!" She was getting really excited and I wondered if the people at the tables next to us could hear what she was saying. She continued with stories about the house she lived in with four other striptease girls and the things that happened in the nightclub, in her house, on the plane to Indonesia, etc.

She was telling it all as if in a trance. She paused for a while, clearly transported back in time. She then suddenly lifted her head, her eyes opened wider, and she screamed, "Why did I forget my toolbox! My toolbox! You should see the play tools I have back in Perth!" I am certain most of the restaurant heard it and embarrassed I immediately asked for the bill. Wendy just sat there shaking her head – clearly angry with herself for forgetting something so important to her.

I drove her straight home to her mother's house somewhere on Jalan Fatmawati. She called me the next day, thanking me for the lovely night out and told me that she just accepted an offer to work for an airline in the Middle East. For an entire year I didn't see or hear from her – until she walked into BuGils a year later.

"Hi, how are you! Still working in Saudi?" She looked at me in confusion and replied, "Saudi? No, I just got back from Perth." Now I was the one confused. "You are Wendy, right?" I asked her. "No," she said, "my name is Sheila." A *bule* then wrapped his arms around her from behind, eyeing me with suspicion. She gave me a wink and I got the message. I apologized and backed off. But I was sure it was her. I could never forget the story about the toolbox.

I went up to Uci, the cashier. "Uci, now what is the story about Madura? Do they use sex tools there?" She moved her chair backwards a bit and turned towards me. "Of course," she said: "the most famous is the Tongkat Madura (Madura Stick). It works very well and is safe to use. But I specialize in jamu. When I was ten years old my grandmother taught me how to make many different kinds. They all have the same effect and they also give a special fragrance to the…uuh…, well you know. And yes, some of the grandmothers and mothers teach their daughters at a young age how to make use of certain muscles. There are special ways to train your vaginal muscles and that is also what you learn about at sex gymnastics. But the course is expensive – Rp200,000 for eight lessons a month. But I can tell you it's worth it!"

"You don't happen to carry these Madura Sticks around in a toolbox do you?" I asked her. She gave me a confused look: "Huh? A toolbox?"

Postscript: As a side business, Uci sells bottles of jamu for a mere Rp5,000 with "no side effects".

tour guide leaves group behind

Last night this guy came into the bar looking confused. He had a strange look in his eyes and his glasses were foggy even though it was not raining outside. He sat down next to me, ordered a beer and started to talk. He had heard many stories about the nightlife in Jakarta and he was planning not to waste a single second. It was his first day in Jakarta and he wanted to party. After another beer he told me that he worked for a property consultancy in Amsterdam, and was entitled to six weeks annual leave. When he saw a job offer for a tour guide in Indonesia he decided what to do with his holiday. He figured he could take this job and make two Java-Bali overland tours in six weeks. Then he would resign and go back to his old job again! It must have been a very low budget travel agency as he was easily hired. He still couldn't believe it himself, he told me with a big smile.

And here he was, for the first time in Indonesia, with thirty tourists back in a hotel somewhere in the Jalan Jaksa area. I asked him why he did not take the group with him on his night out. The tour guide shook his head again. "I told them Jakarta is a dangerous town and that they had better stay in and around the hotel. I also told them that they should not use ice cubes in their drinks." He took a few large gulps from his beer and continued, "The fact is that I don't want to be bothered by them on my nights out! Ha, ha! Give me a break! They can bother me once we are in the jungles of Java. There is jungle out there, right? But, tell me, what is the best place to go to tonight?" I knew what he was looking for and gave him some directions to Blok M.

He finished his beer quickly and was off into the dark and, according to himself, "dangerous" Jakarta. I don't know what happened with him after he left BuGils but he must have been an easy victim for the "*kupu-kupu malam*". I was more worried about the group he was supposed to lead. If anyone happens to see a group of tourists wandering around the Jalan Jaksa area, please send them to BuGils and I will offer them some free pitchers of beer – without ice.

whoever …

I have this cleaning woman who comes to clean my apartment a few times a week. I now understand why she sometimes didn't show up during the run up to the elections. I was lying on the sofa watching *Cheers* while she was ironing my clothes.

She told me that she had joined the *kampanye*. "Oh really! What party did you join?" I asked her. "Three parties, mister" she answered calmly. "Golkar *bagus*. They paid Rp50,000 for my husband with his motorcycle. I received Rp30,000 for riding on the back. Not bad hey, mister? Megawati also *lumayan* (not bad). They gave us Rp50,000 for both us to come to a rally in the back of a taxi. But PAN? Nah … *pelit*! (stingy) Only Rp10,000 mister!" She had clearly enjoyed the extra income she had received from her involvement in the political action on the streets. She went on to explain the process to me, about the middleman who came to the *kampung*, the registration process, etc. It was a profitable period for her and her family. She had enjoyed the elections. Then, on election day itself she didn't show up for work. I assumed that she took the whole day off to cast her vote.

When she returned the day after the elections I asked her about her vote. "No, I didn't vote. *Hujan* (rain), mister. I had family visiting and it wouldn't make any difference anyway," she added, while cleaning the floor. And that was it – no further discussion. For her the elections were over the moment she received the meager Rp10,000 from the PAN middleman. She considered the government regulation that Election Day should be a day off as a bonus.

There was no need to teach her about the importance of voting. It was too late anyway. There are probably a lot of things in her life that wouldn't make a difference to her – like knowing my name for instance. Until today she still calls me "mister".

Cheers is on TV again. Norm Peterson walks in and everybody shouts: "Norm!" She just turned on the vacuum cleaner. I want to tell her to wait, but I realize shamefully that I don't know her name either. She has already worked for me for a year now. I pay her Rp30,000 a day. For another Rp20,000 I could also have her husband on a motorbike, but naah…. Knowing her name wouldn't make a lot of difference at this point anyway. I had missed the opening joke on *Cheers* already. I silently lifted up my feet.

bugils a gay bar?

Last Saturday I went to BATS in the Shangri-la Hotel and had an unpleasant experience in the toilet. While I was taking a pee, there was this big, blond *bule* standing next to me doing the same thing. While doing this, he used one hand to make a call with his handphone. "Why don't you come here?" he said to his friend on the other end of the line. "There is a good band playing here and there are lots of women!" After a few seconds of silence, he continued: "BuGils? BuGils? That little shithole in Taman Ria!? No way, man! That's a terrible place!"

I was shocked hearing this fellow talking about my bar in this way! I couldn't believe it! I am not easy to shock, but this guy had called BuGils the worst place on earth – loud and clear! Gasping for air I wanted to say something, to defend BuGils. I wanted to hit him, to piss on his pants, anything, but I calmed down and decided to take a more diplomatic approach.

"Hey, I don't know you, but BuGils is not *that* bad. It's actually a pretty cozy place. My best nights out always start in BuGils!" He put away his phone and turned to go to the sink. He looked down at me for a second and said: "Are you joking!? It's a tiny, shitty place. Cozy? Yes, warm and cozy for sharing your food with big fat rats from that stinking lake." I was stunned and highly irritated by now.

At that moment my friend Pieter walked into the toilet. Finally some support. "Hey Pieter, this Dutchman here doesn't like BuGils. It's not that bad, is it?"

"BuGils? BuGils is a gay bar! It's a damn gay bar!" Pieter shouted while hitting me hard on the shoulder, almost knocking me into the urinal. Then he laughed loudly. There were four or five people in the bathroom and by now they were all looking at me. I closed my zipper and, heavily defeated, turned for the exit. On the way out, the Dutchman looked over his shoulder, and with a grin on his face, made a parting jab: "*Ahaa*. Is *that* why you like the place so much?"

Needless to say, Pieter's BuGils Bucks are no longer valid.

peanut sauce

When I came to Asia for the first time in 1990, I was planning to backpack my way to Australia. As I was a low-budget student at that time, I booked the cheapest airline available: Iraqi Airlines. It became a costly mistake. While I was traveling in Indonesia, Iraq invaded Kuwait and Iraqi Airlines stopped flying that same day. I was stuck in Indonesia, waiting for dad's money to buy a new return ticket. Australia was not an option. Fourteen years later, I finally made my first trip to Australia. The trigger for finally booking the ticket was after a regular conversation with a waitress in Taman Safari. While it was Saddam who made me stay in Indonesia, it was this waitress who made me leave for a reality check:

"*Mau makan apa*, mister?"

"Uuh…nasi goreng, but the egg should be well done."

"Sorry mister, cannot. Nasi goreng is with the egg *setengah matang*."

"Well, can't you cook it a bit longer?"

"Mmmmh…*coba*, I will ask the cook…but I don't think it can be done."

I asked the babysitter what she wanted to eat.

"Nasi goreng *juga*, but only a small portion."

"Sorry, *mbak*…cannot. Our portions are standard. Half a portion cannot."

The babysitter and I both looked in disbelief at the very calm waitress.

I decided to have something special with my nasi goreng.

"Can I have a portion of peanut sauce with my nasi goreng?"

In a monotone voice she rejected my request again.

"Sorry mister, peanut sauce *tidak ada.*"

"But you have gado-gado, right?"

"Yes, mister. We have gado-gado. Mister wants gado-gado?"

"No, I don't want your gado-gado, I only want some peanut sauce. Gado-gado is with peanut sauce, right?"

"Yes, mister."

"So you do have peanut sauce?"

A few seconds of silence followed. I could almost hear her brain grinding along.

"Yes, mister, we have peanut sauce. So you cancel the nasi goreng?"

"No! I still want my nasi goreng but with some peanut sauce!"

"Oh, mister *mau* peanut sauce on the side? I will ask the cook. *Itu aja?*"

I went home and booked a ticket to Australia.

counting sandals

I live just behind the new Semanggi mall. In the first weeks of operation only Starbucks and Giant supermarket were open. Every day I watched the laborers passing by going to work on the shops inside. One day, while I was enjoying my Starbucks coffee, I noticed this young Indonesian guy. A teenager, probably just out of high school, he was sitting in the opposite corridor taking notes. It must have been his first job. He always nodded at me in a shy manner, but I couldn't figure out what he was doing. It bothered me.

So after a few days, while this guy was staring at me as usual, studying the *bule* trying to recover from another night in BuGils, I decided to find out of why he was taking notes on me. I put my coffee mug on the table, pushed my chair back and walked up to him. The guy was shocked when he saw me coming resolutely in his direction. He quickly jumped up while looking right and then left as if he was searching for help. He clenched his writing pad close to his chest and opened his eyes wide open.

"*Lagi ngapain?*" (What are you doing?) I asked him. Again he looked right and left as if for help and then stuttered: "*Maaf* mister, I am taking notes on the persons visiting the mall." He offered me a look at his notebook. He was indeed collecting visitor profiles. It was ten o'clock in the morning and so far 99 out of 100 visitors were males wearing sandals. There was only one visitor not wearing sandals and that must have been me. The rest, of course, were only the workers, as the mall was still under construction!

What was the management planning to do with his profile? Maybe they were trying to impress Ace Hardware? Or did they want more sandal shops in the mall? Whatever it was, I told the boy to tell his boss that it was useless at this point. Of course, it was not my business, but for me it was another annoying example of uselessness. I went back to my coffee. The shocked boy slowly slid down to the ground again with his eyes still wide open. I nodded again in a friendly way to the young boy, but he just stared at me. Workers with tools kept on passing by but he didn't count them anymore. He just sat there staring. The next day he was no longer there.

Weeks later, after I had already forgotten about the survey, the guy was suddenly back! There he was again, with his writing pad and an enormous smile! This time he didn't nod at me. Instead he waved to me with his writing pad high in the air! I don't know what had happened, but maybe he had informed his boss that profiling was useless at that time, and maybe, just maybe, he was complimented for his intelligent insight. The mall by now was in full swing. There were fewer workers and the number of shoppers was increasing by the day. I guessed that now the survey was justified.

Coming to BuGils later that day, I sat down and ordered a beer. Then I noticed this message written on the beer coaster: "It's a sad man who drinks alone." This message from the beer coaster was not encouraging. The beer company, that holy institution, was telling me that I was a sad man! I felt like that boy in the mall – sad and useless. I asked for another coaster. This one read "Strangers plus Bintang equals Friends." So I asked for another one. It was similar: "Friday is not Friday without friends!"

"What is going on here?" I thought to myself. I must be the biggest loser in the world! I called the Bintang office and asked them what the idea was behind these messages. They politely answered: "We are aware of it sir. We are taking the coasters off the market." The labels on the bottles still read: "Best Served with Friends." That is fine for us lonely drinkers. After a few beers we can't read the small letters anyway.

feeling important

After fourteen years in Indonesia, I finally made it Down Under. When I arrived in Perth, I immediately caught a taxi to the Northbridge area. After a kilometer or so, the driver, keeping his eyes on the road, started talking. "You are the guy from BuGils, right?" I was shocked. "I read your newsletter. It's a cracker!" he continued. This was the first person I had met in Australia and he knew me. Incredible! Sometimes I like to brag about how I get recognized in different corners of Indonesia, but in Perth…that was a different story! It turned out that the man used to work in Indonesia but moved to Australia with his Indonesian wife nine years earlier, and has been a fanatical reader of my newsletter for years.

The trip to Western Australia was a great escape from the stress and pollution of Jakarta. Great food, clean air and beautiful countryside just a four-hour flight from Jakarta. So through my newsletter I organized a drink with a few of the 'old' Jakarta expats who now lived in Perth. Soon the stories of Jakarta in the Tambora days filled the room with laughter. The best part was that there was one person they all knew: the crippled old lady who used to beg in front of Tambora. Nowadays she has her spot outside Oscars.

Raymond, a Jakarta expat from the 1980s, insisted that

the crippled woman could actually walk. The others were not sure. "When I came back after five years, she stood up and hugged me with open arms! It was unbelievable that she still recognized me!" he shouted. "She only pretended that she recognized you. She does that with everybody!" laughed John. I promised them that I would investigate the matter the next time I went to Blok M.

As it turned out the crippled lady crossed my path, literally, only two weeks after my return from Perth. I had gone out that night with a European ambassador. He is the only ambassador I know of who visits a bar at least once every two days. At the end of a good night out, he decided to go home and told his driver to drop me wherever I wanted to go. It was two AM and I decided I wanted to be dropped in Blok M.

The street was packed. Expats were everywhere, hopping from bar to bar. A large number of Blok M girls were eating in one of the food stalls alongside the rows of parked cars. Sleazy drivers and local thugs were sleeping on the hoods of some of the most beat-up taxis in the entire city. Out of nowhere I arrived in this limousine with its CD 01 license plate and the proud flag of a nation (that I cannot reveal) waving in front. We came cruising slowly down the street. People jumped up everywhere! Police saluted me! Girls stopped eating, Indomie hanging out of their mouths. I could see the surprised faces of expats wondering from what country this ambassador could be. An ambassador in Blok M? In front of My Bar the security guards quickly tried to move all the motorbikes out the way to make a parking space for the approaching CD 01.

I enjoyed the commotion so much I almost decided to go for another 'triumphant tour' through the street, but nah, that would be abuse. In front of Oscars Pub I delicately stepped out the car. "It's Mr. BuGils!" I heard one of the security guards shouting out in surprise. Others clapped their hands. "Hey, Mr. BuGils! *Udah enggak miskin lagi ya!?*" (you finally made some money, eh?) one girl shouted. "*Sekarang aku mau deh sama kamu!*" (now I'll let you take me home!) yelled another. Suddenly, this ancient, toothless begging grandmother rose up from the darkness of the street side and hobbled towards me with her arms wide open. I barely had time to escape her grasping claws and dived into the bar. I don't think she recognized me from the newsletter, like that taxi driver in Perth did. Well, whatever the case, one thing is for sure: she can walk!

saving face

Every two years, for either the World Cup or the European Cup, we set up a stadium on the terrace in front of BuGils. The stadium is eight rows high and can hold about three hundred people. We've been very fortunate to get sponsorship from both Telkomsel and Bintang, and the stadium is always a big hit with football fans.

The day before the opening game of Euro2004, I received a panicked call from the General Manager of Taman Ria. He told me that there would be another event in the complex the following evening and I had to immediately tear down the tent that covered the stadium. The management was furious that one of the poles supporting the tent was placed in the middle of the main entrance. I had to admit that there was indeed a pole there, but in Jakarta there are obstacles everywhere in the streets. I couldn't imagine that it would cause any trouble for the six thousand guests they were expecting so I ignored the complaint.

The next morning it became more serious. The pole had to be moved. A meeting with all the parties involved took place a few hours before the opening. There were ten people around the table, all clearly under stress. Their eyes were all nervously looking in my direction. I could hear them thinking: "How do we deal with this little *bule* and his *keras kepala* and get that damn pole moved?"

The event organizer started the meeting by thanking me for coming and for my co-operation so far. I nodded and enjoyed the few seconds of silence after his speech. They were all sitting on the edges of their stools. I decided to play it in a Javanese way. In a calm voice I thanked them also for this and that and that. I told them that I was sure we could come to a solution. They all nodded with relief.

Then I reminded them that such an event would not bring me extra business. It would mean difficult parking, people using the BuGils toilet, making a mess on our terrace, etc. They all understood this. But they considered the path in front of BuGils to be a bottleneck and argued that the pole could add to the risk of an accident. The construction manager tried to convince me that I didn't need a tent to protect my mini-stadium from rain: "We have asked the help of a *pawang hujan* (rain mover)."

The event organizer and Taman Ria managers all nodded their heads in agreement. "No worrieees, Mr. Bart! No rain lah." "Well, in that case…," I leaned forward. They also leaned forward. "If a *pawang* can move a huge rain storm away from Taman Ria," their eyes were focused sharply, their jaws tense, "and you pay him millions of rupiah, then I am sure for a few hundred thousand extra he can easily make that pole disappear for a day, no?" They slumped back in their chairs, shaking their heads in disbelief. I wanted to cheer in victory, but wisely kept my emotions to myself.

To save face, they came up with the solution. I could leave the pole – and thus the tent – but I had to provide a light on it so that people could easily see the pole. Satisfied, I praised them for their clever solution.

uncovered

That Pak Arif is a funny guy. Once, on one of our company outings, he became a hero. It happened when we were on a staff outing to Pelabuhan Ratu, a coastal village on the south coast of Java. We were at the point of leaving our guesthouse, all twenty of us already sitting in the bus, when I realized that my handphone was missing. Everybody panicked! The boss' handphone was stolen! All the bags were unloaded from the Big Bird bus and the senior staff checked them one by one. I was sure I still had the phone in my hand just an hour earlier!

The staff now became suspicious of the male employees of the guesthouse who were silently looking from a distance at this funny scene. They were sitting on a roadside fence, smoking kretek and watching thirteen sexy Jakarta girls, seven nervous cooks and one confused *bule* trying to locate a missing phone. The search continued to the now vacant hotel rooms and after that to the rooms of the employees. They co-operated, silently spreading out their few belongings in front of their rooms.

Meanwhile, in the reception office, Pak Arif carefully unfolded his holy *keris* from its linen wrapping. He took his shirt off. Then moving the little *keris* around his head, he went into a trance. Soon he started to sweat heavily and the movements of the *keris* became wilder and wilder!

He brandished it dangerously through the air, nearly cutting off one of his ears! But then he slowed down, and with the *keris* in front of him, walked straight back to the bus.

Some of the girls, who were waiting in the bus, now became nervous as the missing phone could be in the possession of any one of them! But Arif passed by all them and went straight to my seat at the back. He then came out of his trance, cleaned the sweat from his face with the palm of his hand and announced his conclusion: "It must be around here somewhere!" But I assured him that we had already searched my bag, my seat and everything. One of the cooks then picked up my sports shoes that were lying on top of my bag. He held them upside down and the handphone dropped out of the shoe.

There was much laughter and relief from the staff. Everybody was happy that there was not a thief amongst them. I was embarrassed and apologized a thousand times to the staff of the guesthouse. Stupid mister Bart. After a delay of more than an hour, we finally continued on our way back to Jakarta. I was impressed by Pak Arif and his paranormal capabilities. True, I should have been much more careful, but I still couldn't remember putting the handphone in my shoe. Why should I have? Pak Arif just winked at me and said, "*Orang bule kurang introspeksi diri?*"* Maybe!

But a few kilometers further down the road I noticed that my handphone was switched off. Who had switched it off? And this was the point. I really was not sure anymore if I had overlooked it, or if somebody had silently put it back while everybody else was turning the guesthouse upside down. Who knows. Sometimes, in Indonesia, there is just no point in trying to uncover the truth.

*Girls in Indonesia have different ways to deal with stress. One way is to cut their hair short. Another way is to stay at home for a period of time of "*introspeksi diri*" or "self-analysis". Over the past couple of years I have heard more and more bar girls use this term about themselves but recently is it common to hear them advise *bules* like myself to do the same thing. Apparently, this lack of self-analysis is the reason we often do stupid things and get into trouble.

pantai hawaii

Have you ever heard about Pantai Hawaii in Bali? Once, I met a Balinese girl who told me that there is a place not many people know about. She told me about a white sandy beach called Pantai Hawaii. Apparently Pantai Hawaii is an isolated beach, hidden below cliffs and miles away from the nearest village. Single Balinese have been going there for centuries to find a partner and to have sex on the spot. Apparently, everybody on that beach walks around naked and people are having sex everywhere! Its an amazing story and I never really thought it was true until this old Balinese *dukun* in Denpasar also told me about it. So on my last trip to Bali I decided to do a little research.

Together with a few regulars from BuGils, I asked around about it while we were in Kuta. Nobody had ever heard of Pantai Hawaii and my friends were sure it was a myth. But, as always, if you ask long enough you can find someone who says he has heard about such things. So I happily embraced this taxi driver who said he knew where it was and would drive us there.

The driver took us to this place where Tommy Soeharto had forced farmers off their land so that he could build a massive luxury housing project. The roads had been built but the project was halted some years ago, just before Tommy went to prison. Groups of these farmers tried to collect tolls from the few tourists who passed through the area, while handing out pamphlets protesting their eviction. "Is this the road to Pantai Hawaii?" I asked them. "Yes, yes!" they shouted and in my excitement I gave them some extra rupiah.

After a few kilometers, we arrived at a group of small bars and surfer hangouts that were well-hidden under the cliffs. The place was called Dreamland. Except for a few stoned Aussie surfers, the beach was deserted and there were no signs of the activities we had hoped for. And, of course, the taxi took off and left us stranded there. I was absolutely sure that some part of the myth was true as two different people, both full-blooded Balinese, had by now told me about it. We sat in one of the bars and I asked the bartender if he had ever heard about the beach where everybody has having sex.

The bartender stared at me for few seconds, and before I realized what an absurd question it really was, he shook his head and put a beer in front of me. He pointed to an old man who was sitting under a nearby palm tree smoking a cigarette and said: "That is a wise man. He should know."

I walked up to the man and asked him if he had ever heard of Pantai Hawaii. The man was dressed in a sarong and had this *dukun*-like expression on his face. His eyes stared into the distance. "Is it a white sand beach?" he asked. "Yes, yes!" I nodded my head. I was sure we were getting closer now. The old man stood up slowly and walked towards the ocean. Standing there in the waves, he looked up and down along the shoreline. Then he walked back to me, sat down and continued to stare out into the distance.

He whispered, "Pantai Hawaii…Pantai Hawaii… *mmmmm*." In a very serious and conclusive tone he said, "Maybe you should go to *Pulau* (island) Hawaii. I think you have more chance finding a *Pantai* Hawaii on *Pulau* Hawaii!" My friends rolled around on the beach with laughter. Without changing the expression on his face, he slowly re-positioned himself under the tree.

happy happy!

There is this new Scot in town who asked me to take him to a 'clean' massage parlor. As it was Saturday afternoon and quiet in BuGils, I thought it would be a nice opportunity to leave the bar for a change and do some 'sight seeing' myself. After strolling through some dodgy alleys around Jalan Hayam Wuruk, we stopped at a place named Mustika. A Chinese man and his wife were sitting behind a counter covered with faded pictures of middle-aged women. A few of the photos had tags on them that read "*ada*" or "*tugas*" (available or occupied).

The moment we walked in, the owner jumped up and shouted: "Hey, my brother!" He tried to give me a high five but missed. I figured he was drunk. Then I looked around and saw the most remarkable collection of creatures. Two men where lounging on the sofa trying to sing along with the karaoke TV. In a corner next to the door was this character wearing a black shiny wig. He looked like a Native American warrior, sitting motionless and cross-legged on a chair. His fat belly was only partly covered with the two remaining buttons on his shirt just keeping it together. He kept making the same movements: raking his left hand through his wig and causing it to shift to the left, then slowly grasping his black beer and taking long swigs. A few other men were trying to keep each other standing or trying to dance, it was hard to say which.

I told my friend that it was not a 'clean' massage place, but he didn't really care. The owner stretched out both arms to him and shouted "We are family!" So we ordered a beer. The beer was served by this amazingly good-looking and well-dressed girl called Vitri. She served the beer with a quiet smile. She was a stunning beauty amidst all the hopeless but friendly creatures around us. Every few seconds we had to yell out cheers with the rest of the group.

A few ladies came down from the massage rooms on the second floor. Vitri kept on looking at me from behind the bar with an expression that seemed to ask "can you please get me out of here?" The Scotsman, new as he was, tried to explain to the girls about his home country, about his experiences so far in Indonesia, and about the differences with Aberdeen. The girls couldn't be bothered but he didn't notice. I heard them repeating "*imut-imut*!" (cute!) Then this large Indian came down the stairs, obviously not happy with the services of the lady he had booked. "Straighten your girls out!" he shouted angrily. The Chinese owner jumped up again and shouted "No problem! No pay! Free! We are happy!" You just had to love this guy. His face was all smiles and he had no worries whatsoever. He was having a good time. He turned to us and with his glass up in the air, cheered again.

The Indian said he would not come back until the owner improved the quality. "Absolutely!" the owner replied. But when the man left, the Chinese owner bent forward and said seriously to us in a whisper: "Bombay *gila*!" Then he jumped up again and started shouting: "We are family! Happy! Happy!" After a few more beers we were all singing along with the karaoke machine – except for the lonely guy with the wig who was sitting motionless in the corner.

After an hour of drinking and singing we decided to leave and promised to come back for an actual massage someday. I gave the owner my card and he promised to visit BuGils. The next day he called me. "Hello my brother! Election day no problem! We are open! And we are happy! If you come, it is free! You are my family!"

Postscript: A few months later we did go back for that massage. Nothing seemed to be different since our first trip: the wig man was still sitting cross-legged and playing with his hair. The owner was still happily drunk. The only thing missing was Vitri and I asked him about her. With a sad look on his face, he glanced at the empty seat behind the bar and explained "Vitri was not so happy here…" Then he shrugged his shoulders and shouted with his glass held high: "But we are happy!"

devil possession in yogyakarta

The first night of the staff outing to Yogyakarta almost turned into a nightmare. Along with eight of the female BuGils staff, I went to this little cozy bar on Jalan Prawirotaman. Hoping to discover some new recipes for our own bar, we tried all the different cocktails on the menu. Before long, the girls starting singing and dancing and even dared to challenge me to a few shots bottoms up. It was not my intention to get everybody drunk, but we all had a great time. And hey, the drinks were cheap.

Later that night we stumbled into *becaks* and returned to the colonial-era Hotel Garuda. I went straight to my room. Behind me I heard the hotel management trying to calm the girls down. An hour later I could still hear them singing and laughing. Then, just when things had finally gone quiet, I heard a loud scream. A short silence was followed by another scream! Now things went crazy and all my girls started screaming and shouting in panic! I quickly ran to their rooms.

It was the most bizarre scene. There, in room 516, Riri was in a wild and violent trance and acted like she was possessed. She had had quite a few drinks that night, but this was not drunkenness, nor something put on to scare everybody. She had absolutely no control over her howling and contortions. She was even trying to claw at the other girls. They were in a total panic! Some of them were crying in the corridor. Our *dukun*, Arif the cook, came to the rescue. He took a little *keris* in both hands and went into a trance. He quickly managed to calm down our waitress Riri, but just as she returned to normal, Rini became possessed! Due to all the commotion, all twenty-three staff and many of the guests were now wide awake.

Now Rini was swinging her arms around in the air and shouting at the people around her. Arif was now in such a deep trance that beads of sweat were rolling down his face. He held his *keris* firmly out in front of her while he chanted in old Javanese. As soon as Rini calmed down, another girl, Catry, ran to the bathroom and started vomiting. For a second it looked if she was going to go into some kind of devil possession as well. But Arif swiftly moved his *keris* in her direction and prevented it. Finally, everyone was back to normal.

The kitchen boys started making jokes again and the girls, much relieved, went back to their rooms. According to Arif, the spirit in room 516 had been disturbed by the racket the drunken girls had been making. Nobody dared to stay in room 516 for the remainder of our stay.

a jakarta bar in singapore

When the new Singaporean Prime Minister announced that he would loosen up the licensing laws, I instantly had this new idea: a Jakarta Bar in Singapore.

At this bar we would serve sop buntut and soto ayam, and of course Bintang on tap. The staff would be brought in from Batam or Jakarta. There would always be smiling faces behind the bar. It would never be boring. A uniformed *satpam* would guard the door and a *preman* would manage the parking in front of the premises.

One task of this *preman* would be to create chaos in the street every afternoon so that a real "*macet total*" can add to the illusion that you are actually in Jakarta. When you order nasi goreng, the staff would inform you one hour later that it is *habis*. Then you would order mie goreng but you will get a nice portion of chicken saté instead. You might drink coffee tubruk, but your bill will show a double whisky. You might go mad, but the staff will just smile at you and say "*Maaf*, pak. *Aku masih baru*!" (Sorry mister, I'm still new). But you would think, "yes, this is Jakarta!"

Who will come to this bar? Mainly expats who have lived in Indonesia and who are now based in Singapore. There are thousands of them. You can actually recognize them when you go to the toilet. They are the ones who open their pants all the way, lift their shirts up to their chins, and hold them there until the job is done. Talking about the toilet, for sure we will print footprints on the toilet seats! Another group of customers will be the thousands of *pembantus* living in Singapore. A lucky draw and a free coke will get them in.

At the end of the night, when you have settled the bill after re-counting it numerous times, you will order a taxi. Don't worry, the Prestasi driver will bring you home safely – eventually. He might drive around a bit, but come on, we want you to get the Indonesian feeling! And don't mind the meter, it won't work. This will be just to keep your *tawar menawar* skills sharp.

The next morning you will wake up with a splitting headache, no doubt because of the pirated Jameson whiskey we used for the mixed drinks. And if you indeed are to go through the total "Jakarta experience" you will have next to you a girl who will be typing non-stop text messages on her handphone with one hand while holding out the other hand for taxi money! From the moment she refuses the Singapore Dollar equivalent of Rp10,000, you will realize that the "Jakarta experience" is over. A Jakarta Bar in Singapore? Well, if the new Prime Minister is serious about loosening the place up, I would love to give it a try.

love liquor

It was a quiet Monday evening and already late when they came in — two well dressed office girls who proceeded to seat themselves next to me at the bar. With a few die-hard regulars staring at them from the other side of the bar, they probably didn't feel like staying, so I figured they could use some "love liquor" to lighten up their evening. This love drink is a sweet green liquor in an enormous tall bottle. The girls looked skeptically at the label which read: "Warning. Consuming this alcoholic liquor can have a shocking effect on sexual inhibition."

I warned them that even if they just smelt the green fluid, they would become "*panas*" and "*bergairah*" (hot and horny). "Just a little sniff of the liquor will make you want to have a man. It is better then Madura jamu!" I said. The office girls were not impressed. "Yeah, sure" they responded. "OK," I said, "then just leave the bottle. It is better that way. I don't want to have you raping my customers later on." They looked at the other side of the bar at the gloomy-looking regulars and started laughing. "We don't think that will happen," they replied.

The girls started focusing on the bottle again. They now both had their hands grasped around the long neck, slowly moving them up and down. "You see!" I shouted. "The love effect has already started while you are just looking at it!"

They laughed until a regular from the other side of the bar started to get involved. "Hey, Bart. You've got that love stuff out again? Don't give that to them, man. They are so innocent. You know what happened last time you did that!" I agreed and decided to put the bottle back again on the shelves.

Before I could put it back, one of the girls quickly unscrewed the cork and took a deep sniff. "No! Don't do that!" I warned. Uh, oh…too late. Everybody was now looking at the girl, waiting for her first response. Her friend asked her impatiently: "How is it? *Ayo*, do you feel anything yet?" A few long seconds followed, then: "Mmm…not yet," she answered calmly. She looked at the other people sitting around the bar and remarked: "They are still as sorry-looking as they were a moment ago."

Then she looked at me. She was a good-looking woman about 30-plus. "No. Sorry. Looking at you doesn't turn me on either." The regulars clapped their hands happily. Then she added: "But I do like the bottle. May I have it?" I asked her: "What are you planning to do with it?" While holding on to the bottle with two hands, she replied in a "Clint Eastwood" style: "None of your business, barman." The regulars were cheering. I didn't ask any further questions and gave her the bottle.

Two days later; the quieter girl came back to BuGils, and asked me if I had more of the love bottles left. "Why?" I asked her. "It didn't work did it?" Then she revealed the truth. "Well, the liquor didn't do it for my friend, but the bottle did. She is a lesbian you know. You and your regulars could make her drink gallons of love liquor and she would never get interested. *Kasian deh, loe*!

cash or carry

"She is absolutely not a hooker!" Jan said while taking a sip of his early morning coffee to recover from his first night out in Jakarta. Jan was on his first visit to Asia and stayed in my house. "By the way, when I told her that my principle is never to pay for women, she just shrugged her shoulders!" Jan was clearly irritated when I advised him to give the girl – who was still upstairs in his room – some money for a taxi home.

"Where did you pick her up?" I asked him. Jan searched his wallet and found a receipt from the night before. He looked as if he had been knocked out. "What is 'Long Island Iced Tea'?" he asked me while looking dazed at the bill from BATS. "Damn. How can they ask so much for a cup of tea?!" he continued. "Long Island Iced Tea is an expensive cocktail. Maybe the *most* expensive cocktail. It only looks like tea," I explained to him. He didn't look happy.

Jan returned to the topic of the transportation fee. "If she doesn't have money for a taxi, how come she has the most expensive mobile phone that is available? She told me she is a businesswoman, selling insurance or something like that." Jan had made his own conclusions. "You have been here too long, Bart. You don't trust the people anymore." I decided to leave the issue alone. Jan quickly finished his coffee and went back upstairs. He was clearly enjoying his trophy from BATS. An hour later the girl came down the stairs. "I will bring you to the road and get you a taxi," I heard Jan say. With high heels she was wearing a short shiny red skirt and black see-through top. I figured she wouldn't sell a lot of insurance policies if this was to be her working outfit for today.

A few moments later Jan returned happily from his 'walk of shame'. "And now I need some sleep. I earned it. She had never experienced someone like me before!" he said proudly while bounding up the stairs in a few large steps. "Sure," I said. I took another coffee and sat back on the sofa again. Then, suddenly, I heard Jan calling me from upstairs. "Bart? Have you seen my video camera anywhere? I am sure it was in my room…."

In the newspaper I saw an advertisement for luxury bags. I held it up in the air. "Hey Jan, look at this. These bags…it is amazing how small they are, but nevertheless they can carry a lot. Don't you think so?" But Jan was already back in his room, continuing his search for the camera. I shrugged my shoulders and continued reading my paper.

the colonel

The last few customers were stumbling out of the bar. Behind me I heard the girls closing the door and shouting back and forth if the air conditioning was turned off and if the empty glasses on the terrace shouldn't go inside. The lake in front of BuGils was peaceful and not too smelly. Another evening in BuGils had passed. Jan (nicknamed the Colonel) had – again – created a commotion earlier in the evening.

About fifty years old, the Colonel had the strange habit to go into war discussions with everybody in the bar. Having enormous respect for the Indonesian Brimob, Police and Marines, he couldn't talk about anything else. He actually claimed he was a marine himself who once fought in Lebanon. Crazy, alcoholic or just weird, he had an amazing ability to upset people. He would walk up to tables were couples were having a romantic dinner, and then tell them to shut up or else…and then slowly move his finger across his neck as if he was going to slit their throats. Apparently he had a job that paid well as he would easily drink ten double whiskeys in an afternoon. And the only way we could get him to leave was if all the staff saluted him and someone would carry his briefcase to the taxi.

Earlier that evening, he was standing quietly at the bar when suddenly he raised one finger high in the air and began shouting "*It* will happen on the first of September!" Willem, a Dutch regular, quietly asked him *what* would happen on the first of September. The Colonel's eyes bulged out of their sockets and he swayed back and forth, as if he was afraid he could be assassinated at any moment. "Quiet!" he screamed and then pressed his finger to his lips. He made the impression that he finally wanted to present his secret of September the first. He stretched his back, took a deep breath, held it for a second, then just shook his head and took a big gulp of his whiskey, then a big gulp of his beer, then a big gulp of his water. Apparently he decided not to share his secret with the bar. A few seconds later he screamed, "They will get us all!" Everybody around the bar, including the staff was now staring at the Colonel. "They'll get us all!" he shouted again. His made his hand into the shape of a pistol and pointed at Willem's head. "Let them mind their own business. They have planned it all. Don't, I repeat, don't get involved!"

I was watching the Colonel's incredible outburst from the other corner of the bar. His bug eyes scanned the room and stopped when he saw me. He pointed at me and yelled, "He will survive! He will survive!" Then he suddenly decided it had gone far enough and made a "forget it" gesture in all directions and went back to drinking his whiskey, beer and water.

Postscript: As we figured, nothing happened on September the first, but ten days later terrorists attacked the World Trade Center. Was this what the paranoid Colonel was trying to tell everyone? Who knows. Anyway, he kept coming back and upsetting customers – so often I actually had to ban him from the bar. He stayed away for a few weeks. One afternoon he called me and wanted to have a chat that afternoon at BuGils. He seemed to have changed his character completely and asked to be given a second chance. Instead of the one whiskey, one beer and one water sequence, he suggested to serve him one whiskey, *three* beers and one water. Is this guy for real? For some reason I agreed but had the feeling it wouldn't be long before things went wrong again.

Sure enough. After a couple weeks on his best behavior he got into an argument with an old regular at the bar. This guy got so upset at the Colonel, he walked out of the bar and collapsed on the terrace. He hit his head and fell into a coma for two weeks. After spending several months recovering at a hospital in Singapore, he was repatriated to the States and will probably never work again. As for the Colonel, I made it clear that it would be better for him and the other guests if he didn't come back anymore. I don't know where he went, but, in spite of all of his flaws, I do kind of miss him. He was certainly a colorful character and the ultimate *bule gila*.

a typical morning

Today I woke up around six o'clock when my two-year old daughter tried to pull me to the TV to watch Teletubbies, a show with the scariest monsters I have ever seen. I tried to sleep on the couch a bit longer, half-disturbed by the "oh-oh's" and "hi-hi's" of Dipsy, La La and Poo. The night before in BuGils hadn't been that busy and I realized that I actually felt good as I only drank water the entire evening. Barely awake yet, I checked my email.

One customer in America is worried he cannot use his old BuGils Bucks anymore now that we have launched a new collection. Another wants to know if the rumor is true that Koi restaurant will be taking over the kitchen in BuGils. Then I check my handphone. There's an SMS from a man who lost his credit card last night. BuGils was the last place he remembered using it before he went to Blok M. There's another SMS from our cashier Uci. It's the sales report from the night before. Not much in the way of sales, but then again, it was only a Sunday. Next there was a missed call from a friend who was having trouble with immigration. I forwarded him a number of somebody who might be able to help. Then there was my mother who had left a voice mail. I normally listen to her message twice; first to hear her message, and then, to hear the familiar sounds in the background: the noisy milking machine, young cows screaming, dogs barking and my father shouting at my brother that he shouldn't do this or that. This time my mother is calling to confirm that she is coming to Indonesia in early October, though without father, who still doesn't want to go on a plane. Father has his own reason: "I don't want to eat nasi goreng for two weeks." Discussion closed.

There is this eighty-year-old farmer from my home village who has asked my mother if he could join her. This iron man, with his large hands and face grooved from seventy years of fighting nature's elements, has worked his whole life on one square kilometer of land. Now, he had suddenly decided to make the trip of his life. I love and respect these kinds of people. Here's a man who has always worked hard, supported the Dutch Resistance in World War II, and has never cheated anyone. He has even been rewarded with an honorable title from Queen Beatrix. I was looking forward to showing him around.

I realized that I had better have some extra money in my account so that I could receive them properly. Right away I prepared a promotion package for an office product so that I could earn a commission. I sent it straight out and a few people responded within ten minutes. It was a good start to the day. Then I had a shower and went off to Starbucks to have a coffee and to write a story for my newsletter. I decided to go to the one in Pondok Indah as I wanted to check out some locations in that area for another BuGils bar. While I was opening my laptop, my assistant called me and informed me about some company which had bought Belgian beer from me. The accountant demanded a commission before he would transfer the payment. I simply told my assistant to stop supplying them. I realized I was talking very loud. I looked up and saw these two older ladies sipping their coffee and looking at me in a friendly way. "You are the *bule gila* ya? From the TV series?" I gave them a slight nod. It is twelve o'clock. The morning is over.

bugils for sale?

Taman Ria recently rented out the main building of the complex to a developer who wants to turn the place into some kind of space-age amusement park. Curious to see how BuGils would fit into their concept, I visited their management office and found a few Chinese men huddled in discussion over some scattered papers. A few other middle-aged professional-looking Chinese women were busy preparing promotion maps. They were all so engrossed in their work that they hardly noticed me at first. Eventually they all looked up and saw me, a *bule*, clearly a prospect for them. A well-dressed executive came towards me. Within three seconds I was sitting down at a table with a plastic Aqua cup and a prospectus map. The glossy prospectus included an artistic impression of the future Taman Ria complex and a layout of the available properties for rent.

"How much space are you looking for?" the salesman asked me. I didn't answer as I was trying to find the BuGils spot on the floor plan. My finger slowly moved over the paper and stopped at the triangular spot that obviously was my little bar. "That's my place!" I expressed in surprise. "Oh. You want that space? That is indeed a nice spot and it has a great lake view." By now, aggressively focused on a sale, he asked: "How many years do you want to rent it for?"

I said: "No, no! That is *my space*!" Jabbing my forefinger at the spot, I yelled again, "This one!" The salesman jumped up from his chair and asked the two ladies for a calculator and started punching in numbers. I was shocked. In the space where the BuGils terrace was supposed to be was written: "Drop off goods." I couldn't believe it. The salesman continued: "That space is a hundred and fifty square meters. Do you think that is enough? What kind of business are you thinking of if I may ask? It is perfect for a restaurant, mister!" I was astonished and replied with more than a hint of irritation in my voice, "But there is a restaurant there now. It's BuGils! You cannot rent it out!"

But the salesman simply started laughing, pressed the off button on his calculator and made my then worst nightmare even worse. "Listen mister. Mister *siapa*? *Maaf*? They will be gone soon. They have finished the contract." I was perplexed. This meathead was trying to rent out the space to me while I still had a contract for four more years!

At that moment a *satpam* (guard) came out of the executive director's office with an envelope in one hand and a big smile. It was the *kepala* (head of) security. He saw me sitting there and came straight towards me, proud to let the Chinese executives know that he knew me. "*Halo*, Mister Bart! *Apa kabar*? BuGils busy *terus*, ya? *Bagus*!" While shaking hands, he whispered proudly to the property salesman, "This is Mister Bart – the owner of BuGils!"

Now the salesman experienced the shock that I was in already. His jaw fell open. He excused himself and said it would be better if I saw the boss. I couldn't have agreed more. The boss came in fifteen minutes later. He was clearly busy. He shook hands with me while continuing to talk on his handphone. The man didn't even look at me. Then, when he had finished his telephone conversation, he turned to me and said: "What can I do for you?"

I told him I was interested to know what was going to happen with BuGils Café. He answered enigmatically that BuGils could sit out their contract and then I could rent the space from them. He was typing an SMS at an amazing speed and had obviously little interest in the discussion. There was not much sense in talking to this guy. I just walked out of the office.

Back in BuGils the staff felt that there was something not quite right with the boss. I showed them the future design, the enormous spaceship that is scheduled to land on Taman Ria. What was their first reaction? "Oh, *bagus banget*! Design *bagus*!" (Oh great! Nice design!) Then, after a few seconds of silence – "Uuuh… *posisi BuGils di mana sih*? (but where's BuGils?)

Postscript: At this stage it is still unclear as to what will happen with BuGils in the near future. The "space" project seems to be moving ahead – barely. Shortly after this meeting, though, several curious events happened: one morning we discovered fifteen centimeters of water in the bar. Apparently a pipe in the kitchen burst the night before. Then, our electricity mysteriously kept going off more often than ever. Funny thing is the guests just got used to drinking in the dark and we considered it business as usual. More sinister, though, is one night when smoke began to fill the bar when it was full of guests. Everyone ran outside the bar and saw some of the space project workers lighting a bonfire in the empty premises directly above BuGils. The staff yelled at them to put out the fire, but workers they were only doing it to kill the mosquitoes. Kill mosquitoes or burn the whole building down? Hmmmm...

kita bisa bantu mister

I received a call from the bar, I had to come immediately. The Bea Cukai (import tax department) was in BuGils checking if all the beverages had an "import duty paid" sticker on them. When I walked in, three men were busy sealing boxes of beer and liquor, and stacking them in a corner of the bar. A large red Bea Cukai sticker made clear they were now 'illegal' goods.

I sat down with the men and one, a Batak, started a non-stop monologue of which I didn't understand much. I couldn't concentrate on the long list of licenses, codes and tariffs he was talking about. For them, it was all part of the procedure to show that they were not just raiding a place and then asking for money. They actually know their business. But nevertheless, in the end, they want money. How often before had I heard the words "*kita bisa bantu*" (we can help).

I thought that they were trying to grab as much as possible before a new president was elected. I gave them some nasi goreng and the discussion went in another direction. They had just swept all the bars in Plaza Indonesia, were now on their way to Mahakam and tomorrow to Cilandak. "But don't tell anybody!" they warned me.

After this disturbing encounter, I went to a meeting of Taman Ria tenants that had been organized to discuss the current problems and the plans for future developments.

Just one month ago, the management had given the fruit shop Buah Segar permission to extend their premises and add a seafood restaurant. Two weeks after the opening of the restaurant, the management informed them that they had leased the space to a developer and told them to close both the fruit shop and restaurant. When Buah Segar asked for compensation, the electricity was cut off. The Chinese owner looked dejected when he told the others in the meeting that all his fish were now dead. Similarly, the karaoke hall, Halte, was also told to shut down within four days and the management had already turned off the air conditioning. Contract? What contract?

TGI Friday's didn't have a supply of clean water and decided to pump it themselves from the underground well. The first morning they tried to use it they discovered that the building management had installed a meter the night before! The manager of the sports bar Frontrow and the manager of the wine lounge Manna House complained about the increasing number of *preman* (street mafia) in the parking lot. They work together with the *satpam*, they said. A fatal stabbing a few weeks earlier, a shooting just before that, and a number of car robberies in recent weeks wasn't good for business. We all agreed. Luckily for BuGils these problems were only on the north side of the complex.

Walking back from Manna House to BuGils my mother called me on my handphone. Her 82-year old travel companion who was coming with her to Indonesia next month had asked her if his 220-volt Philips shaver would work in Indonesia. The old farmer was a bit worried about it. "Everything here works fine, mom, just fine…."

contract wives

I have this ladyfriend in Jakarta who I have known for many years. She is a single parent and her daughter is about two years old, just like mine. She became pregnant after an affair with a Frenchman while on holiday in Paris. When she came back to Indonesia, the Frenchman at first didn't want to have anything to do with the child. When it was proven that he was indeed the biological father, he started sending monthly child support to the mother. But it was already too late. The two-year old daughter, a lovely little girl, was by now calling her father "*papa banci*" (papa ladyboy) over the telephone. The poor child has never seen him. Sometimes, on the phone, she asks him the same question over and over: "*Papa homo Perancis ya? Papa homo Perancis ya?*"

Another form of family support is the concept of the 'contract wife'. It is indeed a service available in Indonesia, though many Westerners don't believe it exists. But over the years I have met a number of expatriates who have had contract wives. The contract wife agency offers you a wide range of women in different age categories. Usually they are in their mid-thirties or forties. Most of them are divorced and have some kids that are taken care of by relatives in the *kampung*. A contract wife will do anything a 'normal' wife does or should do, at least in the old conservative concept of marriage, such as doing the cooking, taking care of the *pembantus*, paying the electricity bills, buying groceries, etc. She will also sleep with you in the same bed, but only if you want. A contract is normally for three years, but there is always the option for an extension. The agency receives a consultancy fee and the contract wife receives a monthly salary. A good-looking wife in her thirties may receive around four million rupiah a month while a lady in her forties gets between two and three. The husband has the option to terminate the contract, but this will result in a penalty.

I started thinking. In BuGils I have met so many men who have tried to set up a business here or who were trying to find a job and failed. Most of them had just one goal – to stay in Indonesia and enjoy the good life. Wouldn't it be a good idea for them to become contract husbands? I think my friend with her young daughter might like to have one. You can probably negotiate a salary in euros.

still going strong

"Don't tell your mother I paid those bastards two hundred euro to get their visas," my father said over the phone while I sat waiting at Soekarno-Hatta airport. My mother and the eighty-year old Frisian farmer would be arriving any time now. My father explained that there had been a lot of stress prior to their departure. They left for Schiphol Airport at four AM. When they arrived, it turned out that their departure was actually in the evening! They had been wondering what 'PM' stood for. But worse still, they were told they could not board if they didn't have a visa which would take seven days to arrange!

The old farmer slammed his large fist on the counter: "I am not going back to my village! I am going to Indonesia!" My father cooled him down. As it was still early and they had twelve hours until departure, they quickly went to the Indonesian embassy in The Hague but they didn't find much help for a quick solution. "These people can actually walk and sleep at the same time!" my mother recalled later. In the embassy, my father came into action. He went through every door he could open. No one could stop him. Two hours later all their documents were in order and they raced back to the airport – arriving just in time to board the KLM flight to Jakarta.

Minutes after my father hung up, my mother and the farmer came through customs. Mom proudly recalled how well father got along with the people in the Indonesian embassy in The Hague and how friendly they were. The embassy staff had told my mother that my father was a nice man and that for people like him they could always arrange something. I could learn from that, she said. Be nice to people and you can get a lot of things done. Sure, but I knew it was the money that had spoken. And I always thought my father never really listened to my stories about corruption. I am sure he believed me now.

My mother and the old man were tired. After enduring the usual *macet* (traffic jam), we finally arrived at my apartment. With a cup of tea by his side and his feet stretched out in front of him, the old man fell almost directly asleep. He hadn't slept for two days. I looked closely at him to see if he was still breathing. Relieved, I heard some soft snoring. I chatted for a bit with my mother.

My mother wanted to know why I was still single. I should find a mother for my daughter Patricia. I explained to her that my life had never been as good as it was now. And, I didn't want to make the wrong choice for my daughter. "Once they are in, it's hard to get them out again," I tried to explain. "But you are thirty-seven, you should stop the wild life and settle down," she lectured. "Mom, in this country a lot of girls prefer older men! In Indonesia it is never too late!" And at the very moment I said that, the old man woke up from his deep, deep sleep. He lifted his chin slightly and with eyes still closed, he said: "Huh!? What was that? Oh ya? Do they prefer old men?" Shaking his head slowly from left to right, and with a grin on his face, his chin dropped down onto his chest. He was asleep again – but this time smiling.

the reunion

In the late '50s, Joop Roorda and his wife sponsored a Papuan kid in Dutch New Guinea (Irian Jaya). Through their church, they regularly transferred money to him until the early '60s when they lost contact. For forty years they carried a black and white picture in their wallet of the little Papuan boy they had once supported. For all these years they had wondered what had happened to him.

Then, a few years ago, Joop and his wife received a call from a Dutch newspaper editor who had been on holiday in Indonesia. While visiting Taman Mini in Jakarta, the editor had met a Papuan who told him that he used to correspond with a Dutch farmer but that he had lost contact with him. They used to write to each other about the differences between Papuan and Friesian pigs and other farm-related things. The Papuan sadly told the editor that he had never had the opportunity to thank the Friesian farmer. It was because of him that he now spoke Dutch and English and had a job in Jakarta. The Papuan still remembered the name of the farmers' village. By an unbelievable coincidence, the editor happened to live not far from the old man's village (my own village as well)! When the editor got back to Holland, he easily tracked down Joop Roorda and naturally the story came out in the local newspapers. The Friesian and the Papuan started writing to each other again. And now, finally, they were to meet for the first time!

I brought Marcel from Irian Jaya and Joop from Friesland together at BuGils. Marcel ordered more than he could eat. When 82-year-old Joop told Marcel that he had survived the crisis in the '30s, the war from '40-'45 and the hungry winter in 1945, Marcel felt the pressure to finish his food (BuGils does not provide doggy bags). He managed to eat all his food but was too full to talk afterwards. All being tired after an emotional day, I decided to give them each a glass of wine. Several glasses later, they were having the time of their life. When Joop almost fell down the steps on the way home, I was lucky to catch him by the arm.

Later that night, Joop Roorda called his wife in Holland. The wine had put him in a good mood and he kept breaking into laughter. "It sounds like you have been in Santema's son's bar!" his worried wife said. "Yes, that is correct! And it is unbelievable how these girls working for him can keep their balance! They are walking around on tiny high heels almost ten centimeters high! The things I see here…my dearest wife, you wouldn't believe it."

My mother told me the next day that I should not give him any more wine, but I think he deserved it.

company policy

I was standing in the bra section of Matahari department store. My mother couldn't figure out her size. When she complained that "they use different numbers here," I proudly showed her the bra size converter on my PDA. "Impressive but useless!" she concluded, as she didn't know her size in Dutch measurements either. Her travel companion, the old farmer Roorda, waited patiently.

Roorda told me he worked his whole life for the milk company Frisian Flag – Friesland's most well-known export. The old folks had only one day left in Indonesia before returning to Holland, so I thought it would be fun to arrange a visit to the factory while they were here. I put a call into the factory and eventually received the company's return call. "Company policy doesn't allow factory visits. Sorry." The old man was clearly disappointed. With a sad face he slowly walked away from the bra section of Matahari mumbling "I gave the best years of my life for that company."

Later, back in my apartment, the old farmer was sitting in a chair with his head hanging down over a newspaper. I was not sure if he was sleeping or reading. But then he raised his head slowly and said, "We have one day left. Why not go to that factory and take a picture with us in front of it? Maybe we can give the security guard one euro

and he will let us in. That's how it works here, isn't it?"
Amazing how much this guy learned about Indonesia in
just two weeks. He looked me hopefully in the eyes while
I replied: "Good idea. We will give it a try, Roorda. We
will give it a try…."

ramadhan

It was a gift from my friends – a beautiful electric guitar with an amplifier. I had just received it a few hours earlier for my birthday and then somehow left it in the taxi on my way home from BuGils. I had lost it even before I had a chance to play it!

The next morning I called all the Kosti taxi pools, but they all replied with the same answer: "*Nggak ada di sini*" (It's not here). "Well, can you check in your administration for the name of the driver with the license plate number B4836SX?" "*Komputer rusak*!" (the computer's broken). "Well, can you call all your drivers over the radio?" "The radio is *rusak* as well, mister! Already for one year! Call the head office *aja*!" I tried the number but to no avail. The phone had not yet been installed.

For two full days we tried to find the driver. Then, while sitting at the bar depressed, I noticed this guy peeking in through the windows. He was wearing a Kosti uniform and had a guitar slung over his shoulder. I jumped up and pulled him inside. After a few beers, a steak and a small sum of money, he left again. I was relieved. But why did it take him three days to bring the guitar back? Did he indeed not discover the goods in his trunk for three days? Or did he first wait to see if anybody would come looking for him before he did the right thing? After all, it was Ramadhan!

That same day my babysitter informed me that she had lost her handphone. She said she had been hypnotized by a person on the street. She had no idea what had happened. Luckily the thief took the handphone and not my daughter. The question is: was she indeed hypnotized? I had heard of similar stories involving hypnosis by con men. Or, had she sold it because she needed money for her family in the *kampung*? After all, it was Ramadhan....

subtle

Since its opening on 1 January 2000, BuGils has never been closed – not even for one day. Every year with Ramadhan, we have to risk staying open, but so far we have been lucky.

A few weeks ago I went for a beer in Jalan Jaksa, at little old bar called Romance. There I ran into Pak Budi, one of the city officials who normally comes to BuGils once a year during Ramadhan to get his yearly payoff. At first I didn't recognize him as he was not wearing his government uniform. I had caught him red faced, not with his pants down, but with a beer in his hands and two young girls at his side. The girls were clearly not colleagues out for an after-work drink. For them, it was a drink before the job.

Enthusiastically I walked up to Budi and shook hands. The girls, in their early twenties, looked up in surprise. In their hands, they both nonchalantly held cigarettes smeared with red lipstick. Budi introduced me to the girls and offered me a beer. "He is the owner of BuGils Café," he whispered to the girls. The girls looked up with their mouths open as if I was more important than the president. Budi then quickly addressed me: "This year, no problem with BuGils. We will help again. Same deal as last year. OK?"

I think he wanted me to leave quickly, maybe he was *malu* with the girls, so I decided to tease him a bit. "Do they work for you? Are they your family?" He only replied with a "No, no, no…" and a shy smile. He started to sweat a bit. "You should bring them to BuGils!" I suggested. "No, no, no…" he replied but the girls liked the idea. "*Iya Om, mau dong, Om*!" One of the two girls started to flirt with me. Her leg made subtle contact with mine under the table. Budi opened the upper button of his tight shirt and took a few quick gulps of his beer. "No problem with BuGils this year, Mr. Bart, no problem…."

sleep with me

The first question Alan asked when he walked into BuGils after being away for several years was: "Is my record still standing?" It was Alan, the Filipino. He was my first regular customer when we started five years ago and he still kept the record for drinking the most beers non-stop: a staggering 158 glasses of beer over a period of two days. I thought it was three days, but he insisted it was two – and don't forget the bottle of tequila. I know most people won't believe it, but he really did it. He was sitting in front of the door at ten o'clock in the morning and drank until closing. He was there again the next morning.

Some four years ago, this character sat down opposite a decent girl who was just sitting there waiting for her boyfriend. He excused himself politely. She didn't see much harm in the little innocent-looking Filipino guy with his hands crossed in front of him. So she nodded to him in her friendly way. Then, in an almost apologetic voice, he asked her bluntly: "Do you want to sleep with me?" The girl opened her mouth and looked at him. "What?" she reacted in disbelief. Alan sat there calmly with his little eyes half-closed: "I want to sleep with you. I think you are beautiful. Is that OK?"

The girl tossed her long hair over her shoulder, smashed two hands flat down on the table for maximum effect and reacted with a furious look on her face: "What? Are you crazy?" Alan did not react. He was completely still. "No. Why? I want you. Tonight!"

The girl looked around in astonishment at the people sitting at the bar. We all quickly looked the other way. She pushed her chair backwards and jumped up. "You are crazy! You are a crazy drunk bastard!" she shouted. Alan didn't give up. "Hey, I can pay you. How much do you want?" The girl took one shoe off and started hitting him on the head with her sharp heel.

At that moment the girl's boyfriend, a British expat, walked into the bar. He quickly intervened and managed to cool things down. His girlfriend ran out of the bar while making a phone call to her father. The Brit urged me to get the drunken Filipino out of the bar because it was quite likely that a truck of marines would arrive within thirty minutes, as the girl's father was a colonel. Like a wounded puppy, Alan was whisked away through the kitchen's backdoor. That was the last time I saw Alan, some four years ago.

On returning to BuGils and looking around the bar for some familiar faces, he exclaimed to me: "A lot has changed here, in these years while I've been away." Only Widi looked up and waved him a kiss. "That's right, Alan," I confirmed, "but don't look so sad. Your record is still standing. Indonesia has a new president. BuGils has a new kitchen. My babysitter has a new handphone. Life is getting better every day." But he wasn't listening to me. He had his eyes focused on a girl sitting alone near the pool table. He ordered a beer and slowly moved in her direction.

Remembering his last exit through the back door and waiting for the worst, I took a long sip of my beer and thought to myself: "Shit. Times change, but some people never will."

wrong strategies

"I have only been back in this country for less than ten minutes and already they are trying to screw me!" my friend said, irritated by something that had just happened to him. Arriving at the airport, he collected his car from the parking area. They wanted to charge him for four days parking while he had been away for only three days. All it took was him spitting out "you damn cheater!" and with a slow "Uuuh …oh yaaaa…*maaf* mister" it was corrected, but it had completely upset my friend. In my opinion there is no way you can survive in this country if you can't control your emotions every time something goes wrong. Too many things go wrong here. It just takes too much energy to get emotional every time. I told him he should have laughed at the guy and said "try again next time!" It would have had been more effective, but that's just my opinion.

Star Deli was ransacked by a radical Islamic mob. Scott (the owner) did the right thing. He cleaned up the mess and opened up again. Then, last Saturday night, around eleven o'clock, three nervous security guards from the complex came to the door at BuGils. "Mister, they are here! In Taman Ria!" "How many of them?" I asked him. For the first time I was nervous, realizing that it could be show time. He replied: "Hundreds! They are now in front of Embassy Discotheque! I bring you there, step on my bike!"

I hopped on the back of his motorbike and we drove around the lake to see what was happening. It was dark and quiet. "The lake smells terrible tonight!" I said over the *satpam*'s shoulder before I realized it was actually the good natured, helpful *satpam* who smelled so bad. Arriving at the front, we found that there was no sign of any problem. Apparently a group of police and government people had been going around warning some bars to close down early. It was a false alarm. I walked back to BuGils through the ruins of Taman Ria reflecting upon how one moment a developer is building a spaceship on the site and the next moment mobs are out with a vengeance wielding swords and smashing up bars.

When I came back into the bar, everybody was anxiously waiting for the news. In the meantime, the regulars had worked out an emergency solution. If a mob of a hundred or so fanatics came our way, they would quickly dress themselves in long white robes and all kneel outside on the terrace. In their new *jilbabs*, the staff would quickly put on some Arabic music. On all the tables they would then put out Bintang Zero bottles and menus with one item – saté kambing. They would cover the pool table with a large black blanket and turn it into a shrine. They had it all worked out and I only had to provide them with one free pitcher of beer as a reward for working out the plan. After a second free pitcher, the regulars were ready to protect BuGils with all means possible. I thought it would be a good idea to put their skills to the test.

So yesterday, I took some big mouth regulars out for a paintball shoot at Mount Putri. Two Americans joined and they were good at strategizing how to conquer the opponents. Their plan was for us to cover them while they attacked. Yet in every game they both got shot in no time! Hey, don't expect much cover from cloggies! And the few Scotsmen that joined, well they hardly used any bullets because they were too expensive. The only participating Singaporean fell into a hole right away, injuring himself and couldn't fight anymore. As a defense force for BuGils, they were all pretty hopeless.

no good, no money back

Tomorrow I am going to Surabaya. I lived there for six months back in 1994. I had this Chinese girlfriend at that time who helped me out a lot. One of the things she helped me with was finding a *pembantu*.

My girlfriend brought me to an old *kampung* on the outskirts of Surabaya. Walking through the little alleys, we arrived at a place where there were many *pembantu* and babysitter agencies. In a number of little houses there, some local entrepreneurs had the poor girls lined up against the walls or seated on old sofas. One agency specialized in girls from Indramayu. I think they did more than cleaning as *pembantus* do not normally wear lipstick in the daytime.

The house next door had girls from Madura, but my girlfriend advised me not to take them. Too many risks involved, she said. I didn't ask any questions. Then, in the next house, I spotted one girl who was young and pretty. My girlfriend noticed my interest as well so she quickly dragged me onto the next house.

I had to make a choice quickly because, in the meanwhile, some fifty people from the kampung, mostly kids, were following us. I decided to choose a big *pembantu*. This girl was from Purwokerto and was strongly built. She looked me fiercely in the eyes. I reckoned she could also function as a bodyguard.

"*Bagus!*" said the broker, relieved when I pointed out my choice. "*Sudah di* training *sebulan*! (She's already been trained for a month) Five other candidates where quickly chased away into the back so as to make space on the sofa for the broker, myself and my girlfriend to sign an agreement. The broker spoke some English: "No good, no money!" he said. I wanted to be sure I knew what he meant: "You mean: no good, money back!" He looked up. "No." Then he looked at me seriously in the eyes. "No mister. No money back. If *pembantu* no good, *pembantu* back." OK. I got the message. "You are a good businessman," I told him, and he proudly swept his signature across the contract.

The *pembantu* in the meanwhile had collected her belongings and was ready to follow. I felt like a rich Roman at a slave market. But in reality I was out of clean clothes and desperately in need of somebody to wash them. I dropped my girlfriend off and I drove home, the *pembantu* still quietly sitting in the back seat. I was dreaming away a bit, received some calls, made some calls and forgot she was sitting there.

Then suddenly, I almost had a heart attack when a voice broke the silence. I was so shocked that for a fraction of a second I thought I had an intruder in my car! I almost slammed on the brakes. I looked fearfully in the back mirror and straight into the tired, sleepy eyes of the new *pembantu*. She had just spoken for the first time. After a silence of three long seconds, she repeated herself, this time very slowly: "*Kalau* mister *minum kopi, pakai gula satu atau dua sendok*?" (When you drink coffee, do you take one or two spoons of sugar?)

127

Positively surprised, my mouth fell open. She was clearly prepared to do a good job. I was happy with my choice already. "One!" I replied with a big smile. In the mirror I saw her head nodding slightly. "One!" I repeated again, but much louder and with a single finger in the air. While she looked dreamily out of the window I noticed a relieved expression on her face. I think she was glad she had been freed from that slave market.

the biggest susu of java

After a round of golf with my Dutch travel companion at the Finna golf course, we did not have much time left to catch the plane back to Jakarta. But my friend had just had a knee operation and the long walk on the golf course had caused him terrible pain. He desperately needed a foot massage as the pain was unbearable. Unfortunately, according to our hired driver, who would turn out to be quite the trickster, all the massage places were closed as it was Ramadhan. However, on the way to the airport, between Malang and Surabaya, I noticed a small sign: "Pijit. Buka". The driver hit the brakes.

The little roadside massage house was smaller than the BuGils toilet. A not-so-bad looking woman of about forty was sleeping in a chair and woke up slowly. She turned out to be the only employee available. I decided to let my friend have his treatment while I waited in the air-conditioned car. We only had half an hour anyway. But the driver of the car, an older and very friendly chap, turned around in surprise. "Why mister no massage?" "There is only one person available," I answered. "I am OK. I will just wait until my friend is finished."

The driver quickly pulled his chair forward, started the engine and said: "No, no! Mister must also have a massage *dong*!" I really was not up for it, not just because we only had half an hour left. But the driver was determined. He probably felt it wouldn't be appropriate if he provided a service for only one of his clients and not the other. He made a dangerous u-turn on the busy Malang-Surabaya highway and raced off to a place that he said might be open.

Again I tried to make it clear that we had to catch a plane, but he wouldn't listen. After about two kilometers he found his destination, another little roadside kampung house with the word *pijit* painted on the window. "*Tidak mau! Tidak mau!*" I kept repeating, but he had already jumped out of the car. Within ten seconds he came back with an enormous smile on his face. "Mister *lihat dulu, kalau enggak cocok, kita balik. Ayo!* (Take a look first, if you don't like it we'll go back) I figured the only way to escape his insistence would be to go in, have a quick look and then tell him, "*tidak cocok*". Slightly irritated, although appreciating his efforts to strive for optimal customer satisfaction, I stepped out of the car and walked into the massage parlor.

It was clearly a place for truck and bus drivers. The little rooms were divided by sheets hanging from the ceilings and the beds were old and shaggy. Three women were lying dreamily on a bed. Through the open door they seductively welcomed me with a slow sultry collective "Hellooo mister!" I quickly turned around to go back to the car. But the driver was speeding away. He had left me behind at the massage parlor. The ladies purred: "*Enak dan sehat!*" "Massage mister?"

One of the three women had already started to prepare a room. Through an open door at the back of the shack I could step right out into beautiful green rice paddies. "I only have thirty minutes," I told the one lady. "No problem. *Buka baju* and lie down." I had no choice. Then she said: "Better two ladies because only thirty minutes. Rp20,000 *aja*!" It sounded like a good deal, so I agreed. She shouted for assistance from somebody in another room. Then she came closer and whispered in my ear – "The biggest *susu* of Java!" Not sure if I had heard her correctly, I could only respond with a "huh?"

Then, through the old dusty curtains, I saw two huge legs coming my way. I looked up to try and see the face of the person coming into the room, but I couldn't. I couldn't see anything. I only saw breasts – huge elephantine breasts! The biggest in Java! It was beyond belief! I could barely make a comment, only *"Ibu punya banyak kayu di depan pintu!"* (You've got lots of wood in front of the door!) The first massage lady was laughing loudly. The big mamma went straight to work and settled herself heavily on my back. Oomph! Then she smacked her hands down on my shoulders. Ouch! I could hardly breathe, let alone move. For some strange reason she kept on asking repeatedly as if she was irritated: "Big *he*? Big *he*?" while the other lady giggled non-stop at the other end of the bed. I couldn't even say yes or no.

Luckily after fifteen minutes I heard the voice of my friend who in the meanwhile had been picked up by the driver. "Bart! Are you ready? We have no time anymore!" I wanted to answer, but the huge lady was still pulverizing my neck and I couldn't say anything with her on top of me. "Mister *belum selesai*!" (not ready) replied the woman on my back. I wanted to shout for help but couldn't. What's more, with three people on it, the bed was making all kinds of creaking sounds and my friend must have thought there was more going on than just a massage. "I'll wait in the car. Whatever you are doing in there, finish it quickly!" he shouted.

A few minutes later I was finally able to escape from under her great weight and iron fists. I was completely buggered. I quickly paid and stumbled back to the car. The driver had a smile of great satisfaction on his face and asked "*Bagus? Enak?*" "*Enak dan sehat,*" I answered dryly. "What on earth happened in there?" my friend wanted to know. I just shook my head and looked out over the beautiful green rice paddies. Amazing nature they have in Indonesia, I thought to myself. There on the roadside between Malang and Surabaya, walking in the footsteps of Wallace and Darwin, I may just have discovered a new species.

wrong room

Last weekend we had the second Jakarta Bar Bash Golf Tournament on my favorite golf course – the Bogor Raya Lakeside. Aphrodite, Mad Dogs and BuGils regulars all competed for a huge silver trophy. Most of the competitors came a night earlier and stayed at the Novotel.

Our most famous regular Huib was one of the participants. When he arrived at the hotel, he was not happy when he discovered that his name was not on the check-in list. Strangely enough, there was a name on the list of BuGils regulars I had never heard of before: Mr. Tong. Huib was angry as he thought I had deliberately not booked a room for him and he wanted to go straight back to Jakarta. Although I wasn't sure, I told him it must have been a mistake. The booking for Mr. Tong was probably for Mr. Huib. After some protesting, he finally agreed to check in under the name of Mr. Tong.

I woke up early the next morning and decided to have a little fun with Huib. I asked the reception to connect me with Mr. Tong's room. It took a while before Huib picked up the phone. I spoke in a very friendly and warm professional voice: "Hello, good morning, reception speaking. There is somebody here in the lobby who wants to talk with you." Before Huib could respond, I changed into Singaporean English.

Loud, angry and fast, I attacked him: "Who are you? What are you doing in my room? You are staying in my room!" Huib was instantly awake. I heard him struggling to get up. His phone fell off the table. "Huh? What?" Huib was instantly disorientated. Next I heard a lamp falling off the table. Pretending to be a highly frustrated Mr. Tong, I continued to verbally abuse our most famous BuGils regular: "What are you doing in my room?! Who are you?!" Huib attempted desperately to collect himself: "No, no, no! It is a mistake! I am not Mr. Tong! I am Mr. Huib!"

Now I started shouting. "Of course you are not Tong! I am Tong! You are sleeping in my room!" "No, No! The organization booked me into this room!" A short silence followed and then I erupted rudely "What organization?" "Uuuh…BuGils! BuGils Café!" "*Bugil*? Huh? Naked?" I took a deep breath and started yelling again. "Are you playing jokes with me? I want you out of my room! Now!" I could hear a totally confused Huib on the other end of the line. "Yes, yes, Mr. Tong! Give me fifteen minutes and I'll be out of here! I am very sorry!" I knew I had to finish the conversation soon as I couldn't hold my laughter in for very much longer. In a final outburst I shouted through the phone one last time: "I am coming to your room right now. Out! Out!" A totally frightened and completely shocked Huib tried to apologize again, but I slammed the phone down on the hook and burst out laughing. For five minutes I cried my eyes out.

Then I made my next move. I went to his room, which was a few doors down the hall. I knocked hard and rapidly on his door. I could hear Huib stumbling and falling on his way to the door. "One second! One second!" he shrieked. He opened the door with one hand raised ready to defend himself. His eyes were wide open, his expression a mixture of fear and innocence. He was hyperventilating. His mouth hung open. But to his initial incomprehension it wasn't Mr. Tong at the door at all. It was that little Friesian bar manager from BuGils. For a few brief seconds he stood there motionless. I burst out screaming with laughter. Utterly defeated, he smashed the door shut in my face.

apples from malang

How do I select my staff? It depends. Sometimes I run into them. Sometimes they run into me. Sometimes I am lucky. Sometimes I am not. When I noticed this very cute looking girl working in Breadtalk, a new and popular bakery chain in a nearby mall, I knew instantly that I had met a likely BuGils girl. When I wasn't sure anymore if I was going there for her or the bread, I gave her my card. A week later she called. She wanted to visit BuGils. An hour afterwards she called again. Could her sister join us? "Sure," I said, "No problem." An hour later she called yet again. Would it be OK if her mother joined us as well? "Sure. Bring her along."

Finally they came: a mother, two daughters and a niece (divorced from a Swedish expat), and her daughter as well. They were all good-looking ladies and they were all very hungry. The mother did the talking. "Which one is the prettiest?" she started, just like that. She overwhelmed me a bit. I didn't expect such a direct question. I looked at her two daughters while they looked shyly into the glasses in front of them. I needed a tactical answer. "They are all *cantik!*" I replied. The innocent looking girl I had met in Breadtalk, and who had by now caused me to put on several pounds, looked relieved and glanced up in my direction. Noticing this, the mother continued, "She has a much darker skin."

Then she pointed at the Breadtalk girl's sister who was sitting next to me and explained: "She is much whiter because I ate a lot of apples from Malang when I was pregnant with her." I didn't feel comfortable with the mother's approach. I was just hoping to meet with a potential waitress. I nevertheless found the apple theory interesting and smelled a story. "Why is her sister darker then?" I asked the mother, who in the meanwhile had started eating her spaghetti. "Because at that time we had moved house and Malang apples were harder to get."

The very modern niece, slugging back vodka, started laughing. She turned out to be a *sinetron* TV star. Showing off how modern she was, she offered her family members some of her vodka, but they refused. Then she ordered a steak for her little daughter. "Mister is paying, *yaaa*?" All eyes looked hopefully at me. I was cornered. I could have said no, because the bill was rapidly rising, but I felt pity for the girl I had initially invited. In her sad and slightly embarrassed eyes I could read an apology. She also didn't like her niece to drink so much (four vodkas already) and was to apologize yet again later when the little girl only ate a fifth of her steak.

Then the mother pointed once more at the darker girl: "She has never been to Bali!" Continuing the conversation shamelessly, the niece added: "She can go with you, if you want!" But the mother quickly interfered. Looking me seriously in the eyes, she said: "It is OK Mr. Bart, but only if I can join in!" The mother and the niece started laughing crudely again. The two sisters simply looked down into their orange juice.

An hour later I politely escorted them to the door, relieved that they were finally leaving. The niece, and what I had believed was a shy girl that I had met a week earlier in Breadtalk, suddenly turned around. Could I help them with some money for their transportation, taxi money. "Sure. No problem." Sometimes you are lucky, sometimes you are not. "Ciputat *jauh*, mister!" Of course. I know.

The next morning I received a call from my office staff. They wanted to know if my exorbitant entertainment bill from the night before wasn't a mistake. It read: "Bill Mr. Bart – table with seven girls." I told them that it was indeed correct. They asked again: seven girls? Again I confirmed the number even though it was only five. They were all laughing. "Mr. Bart *pasti cepat kurus nanti*!" (Mr. Bart will get thin again quickly then!) I couldn't deny it. "*Kurus* and *bangkrut*!" I said and hung up. Maybe I didn't really need an extra waitress for the time being anyway. And besides the bread in Breadtalk is nice, but not so great that I should be buying it every day. Tomorrow morning I will be back on the Indomie...with *telor*. And a table for one.

fat men and young girls

The two girls were only nineteen years old. They had come from Amsterdam and were on a six-month backpacker's trip through Asia. After the usual chit-chat, one of the girls began to express her distaste with the male chauvinism they had encountered in Indonesia. Getting steamed up, she went on to exclaim: "And all these old fat Westerners with these young girls. It's disgusting!"

I had heard it all before from first time visitors. "Well, if both parties are happy, what's wrong with it?" I reacted. The girl stared at me in disbelief and looked over at her friend, who was not particularly interested in the discussion and who was busy downing the dregs of her beer from a pitcher of Bintang. Her friend continued: "Many of these fat old men were probably married before. Did they dump their wives?" I let my own belly sink a bit lower under the table. "Maybe some of them. But it is their lives after all! If a man of 50 is happy with a 25-year old girlfriend, why not?" My defense of fat old men with pretty young girlfriends was useless. "Are you married?" she asked me. She looked at me with a suspicious look, ready to point an accusing finger at me. "No" I said and ordered another pitcher for them, changing the subject before the girl asked me if I was divorced.

It was one of those nights in BuGils when things go

wild – B-52's and tequila belly button shots served up non-stop. Henny was entertaining customers from behind the bar and people had started to dance on the tables. It was two o'clock already and the two blonde girls were still hanging in there. They looked slightly dejected, perhaps for not having received as much attention as the other girls.

When they decided to go home, the two girls came to say goodbye. By now they were in a different mood. One said, "I actually don't want to go home yet, but my friend is drunk already and I don't know where we are going to sleep tonight." "Well…" I said, "you can sleep in my apartment if you want," giving her the response that she had obviously been fishing for. "Oh yeah! Is that possible?" Not forgetting our earlier conversation, I quickly added: "Naah…better not. I am 38 and you are 19. People will talk badly about us, you know." She finished her last glass of Bintang in one large gulp and marched off without saying goodbye.

Then I had a chat with this very pretty Indonesian girl. It was one of those interesting and disconnected evenings. She had just broken up with her British boyfriend. "Why?" I asked her. "Oh, we had different views on life, and different hobbies as well. My hobbies are history and sex. He only wanted to play golf." "Strange," I replied. "Yes, history is sooo interesting," she expounded before asking me, "Did you know that Hitler was actually a very clever man?" She looked at me as a teacher would. I was more interested in her other hobby but she went on about *Mein Kampf*. I didn't let her finish and interjected "Is sex your other hobby?" She confirmed this. "Yes. On the beach.

Oh, I love it on the beach…but did you know that Hitler was actually born in Austria?" I stared at her in disbelief. "Yes, really!" she shrieked. Once again I wasn't connecting with my conversation partner. It was obviously time to go home.

Outside, the two Dutch girls were still waiting for a taxi. Unable to stop myself from playfully antagonizing them I saluted them and cheerily said "Goodnight, ladies!" One of the two turned around, she didn't move for a fraction of a second and then, in a sharp bitchy voice retorted: "Good luck!" "Good luck with what?" I asked. "Good luck with the rest of your life!" Then they quickly jumped into a taxi and left me standing there, thinking to myself, "The rest of my life? What should I do with the rest of my life? Maybe I should look for a new hobby. I don't have one really. Maybe I should start reading history books….

smelly socks

My waitresses have an extraordinary way to make extra money – they sell their smelly socks.

"It's weird," says Riza, who had managed to sell a pair of her socks for Rp300,000 to a Brit regular at BuGils. "The more they smell, the more he pays!" Then Widi excitedly interjects, "a few months ago he paid Rp500,000 for Yayang's sandals." Even weirder, he wasn't ashamed about his remarkable fetish. When he came into the bar, the first thing he would ask me was whether I had any new girls working at the bar. When I did, you could see his nose start twitching.

One night, one of the waitresses was especially excited for, as planned, she hadn't changed her socks for three days. A Heineken in hand, I watched the scene unfold outside on the terrace. She went straight up to him, sat down next to him and said: "Now smell these for something special!" He bent slowly forward, lifted her leg and touched his nose to her feet. Through half-closed eyes, he concentrated and inhaled deeply, hoping to fill his chest with her self-proclaimed especially funky aroma. He took another deep sniff. "Nooo…," he concluded, a bit disappointed, "this is only worth Rp200,000." He paid up immediately.

My bar manager, Adel, who has traveled around the world, laughed and gave me her take on it: "He is British.

I don't know if that has something to do with it, but they like funny things." The Brit has his own explanation. According to him, getting off on socks is safer than having fun in Blok M!

Seeing the front girls making money so easily, the kitchen staff wanted a part of the action as well. Adel was willing to co-operate. After all, Adel was his favorite supplier of smelly socks. As a matter of fact, I suspected that she sold him her underwear as well but was never able to prove it – and why would I anyway? One night I wondered to myself why the kitchen staff were eagerly peeking out from behind the windows and watching Adel at work selling another pair of smelly socks. When she triumphantly came back into the bar, holding several Rp100,000 notes high in the air, I figured out what had happened. Adel was wearing Yoko's socks. Yoko is the dishwasher. Of course she didn't tell this to the Brit. The poor guy had no idea that later, while he was smothering his face in his newly purchased aphrodisiac and having the ultimate orgasm, Yoko and his little family would be celebrating his first sock sale with California Fried Chicken!

Postscript: This Brit continues to be open about his fetish and once explained to me, "You would be surprised. There are thousands of us around." For some reason he didn't show up at BuGils for a while. He probably felt cheated, though who knows how he found out about Yoko. It must have gotten back to him through the grapevine somehow, but whatever the explanation was, he never took the risk of buying socks from the BuGils staff again. Following up on the matter one night, I asked him about his ultimate fetish encounter. It was in Japan were he had his face buried in a pile of socks and underwear. He had four Japanese girls walk all over him until he couldn't bear it anymore. He had the time of his life and paid them 2000 bucks. I thought all along that my staff were selling their socks too cheaply.

free beer for kuntilanak

In a meeting with the other tenants in the Taman Ria complex, the development of the Space Building was being discussed. There were many questions regarding parking spaces, termination of contracts and security. But the person who had organized the meeting didn't show up. The manager was probably lost in space so we continued without him.

"There are lots of ghosts in Taman Ria," said the manager of Halte Karaoke. "They don't allow normal businesses to survive here!" "Absolutely true!" confirmed the manager of TGI Fridays. "Only places with night-time entertainment do well here. All the other businesses have gone bankrupt or have been chased away! It's the mystery of Taman Ria!" Looking around the little circle of about ten managers from the different entertainment spots in Taman Ria, I noticed that everybody was nodding seriously. Mr. TGIF continued: "A salon, a fish restaurant, a fruit shop, the fun park...you name it, they've all gone bankrupt!" "If there is no alcohol involved it won't survive," confirmed the Manna House supervisor.

I had heard of a young female ghost who apparently lived in the sinking ship in the Taman Ria lake. When it was still a floating restaurant, the staff there had often spotted a friendly girl in a long white robe. She would pass them on the stairs on the way to the toilets. The manager of Halte Karaoke said he had seen her a few times in his premises especially "in that one room where everything breaks down continuously. I've had guests come running out of there screaming after suddenly finding a girl sitting next to them!" Other tenants had stories about spirit possession and the manager of Embassy Disco related the story about this maintenance man who caught a fifty-centimeter ghost fish in the lake. I remembered this because I had seen him proudly showing it to his friends. "Well, that guy brought the fish home. That same night everybody in the house became terribly sick. So he decided to return the fish to the Taman Ria lake. Everyone instantly recovered!"

Being the only *bule* in the group, they probably thought that I found it strange listening to all these stories about ghosts, so they asked me: "Did nothing strange ever happen in BuGils, Mr. Bart?" All heads now turned to me as I decided to tell them about the BuGils ghost. Relieved that I didn't find their stories to be complete bullshit, they all bent forward attentively as I explained: "There is this one spot in the bar by the entrance. In the last five years, four different people have fainted there. Just like that. Boom!"

My audience reacted instantly: "Naah! Naaah! You see?" Motivated by their interest, I continued: "Yes, it happened to perfectly healthy people. I myself had weird things happen to me a few times on that particular spot. Once, I couldn't lift my beer. My hand started shaking and I had to sit down!" The manager of TGIF jumped up and exclaimed: "Kuntilanak! It's because that's Kuntilanak's spot

– she's a female ghost! She likes it there. That is why your business is going so well!"

Everyone around the table agreed. I continued: "… and the paintings in BuGils. Every morning, when we come in, they are crooked!" "Naaah!" they all shouted simultaneously. Someone then explained why: "That's because during the night the *hantu* (ghost) sits on the frames!" "What you should do is keep Kuntilanak happy. You should leave a beer out for her every night when you close the bar!"

When I returned to BuGils, I told Widi that every night after closing she should put a glass of beer in the haunted spot. "But when you sit over there…" Widi said, pointing to the corner end of the bar, "you also have this shaking problem sometimes!" "Then put a beer there as well. We don't want to upset Kuntilanak, do we?" Widi pointed again in another direction. "And that spot over there, you…." "Widi, just put the damn beer there, OK!"

Postscript: Until today, Widi puts a beer at that spot at the bar before closing, and we haven't had any more people faint while sitting at her place. We also haven't had any electricity cuts nor floods either. And even our relationship with the Taman Ria management is better than ever! People often ask me if there is beer missing from the glass the next morning. Believe it or not, there is! Come see for yourself – we open every day at 10:30 AM.

a well-planned robbery

I woke to a noisy commotion in the normally quiet neighborhood. I went to the balcony to see what was happening. A group of men were loading a lorry with sofas, a TV, a stereo and other stuff. To my shock I realized they were emptying out the house of my friendly Australian neighbor! He had left a day earlier for Kalimantan but had not told me he was planning to move. Then I noticed his little dark and skinny Ambonese wife running in and out the house. She was clearly in a hurry.

"Are you moving?" I shouted down from the balcony. Bewildered, she looked up at me. I had heard her shrill voice many times in late night fights with her husband when he came home late. "Yes!" she shrieked back. "We have a better deal in Bintaro!" She quickly returned to her work, loading a CD collection onto the truck. I found it strange that he had not told me, but it was too early to think clearly, so I went back to sleep.

A week later, in BuGils, I met my neighbor again. He had just returned from Kalimantan. I could see things were not in order. He was shaking his head and had a desperate look about him as he confided in me, "Every time I left, I would leave the door open, hoping she would walk out of the house and never come back. She never did. But then, when she finally left, she took everything with her! She emptied my whole house! She even took the car!" I realized I had been a witness to this well-planned robbery so I quickly ordered a beer for him and told him what I had seen a week earlier. He looked at me angrily and said, "You know what irritates me most?" I had no idea. "She took all my BuGils Bucks! After three years of coming to your pub, I had an enormous stack! I wanted to give a party, you know…." With a sad face he gazed into his beer. That was two years ago.

Yesterday evening, on my way to BuGils, while I was walking through the front gate of Taman Ria, somebody called my name in a frightening, shrieking voice. Widi and Uci had just bought some food from a roadside stall and were walking ten meters behind me. We looked around in the dark but couldn't see anybody. Then again, the shrieks: "Mister Bart, Mister Bart!" There, behind the fence, I noticed a woman in the shadows. Widi and Uci clung to each other, then, shocked and frightened, they ran off to BuGils. "Mister Bart *ke sini dong*!" (come here) the person yelled, with her hands gesticulating to me through the fence's spikes.

"Who are you?" I shouted back while slowly moving in her direction. She replied with a question: "Is my ex-husband in your bar?" Then I realized that she was my Australian neighbor's ex-wife, dressed all in black. She looked confused and had a strange look in her eyes. "Oh, it's you! No. I haven't seen your husband in ages," I said. She responded nastily "*Mungkin udah mati kali*!" (perhaps he is already dead then!) and proceeded to open a little hand bag. "*Lihat ini* mister!" (look at this) she exclaimed, showing me a huge stack of BuGils Bucks, probably a few hundred of them.

"Can I change this for money? In the bank they told me I could only use them in your bar!" She had been carrying the stolen BuGils Bucks around with her for two years waiting for the opportunity to cash them in. I told her that the BuGils Bucks were useless because they were out of date. Disappointed, she put them back in her handbag, slowly moved back from the fence and disappeared into the dark.

jakarta-bogor: again and again

One of the perks of living in Indonesia is the ability to have domestic staff. Our lives are filled with stories involving drivers, maids, babysitters, gardeners, etc., and it is common to hear *bules* complaining all the time about them. Every once in a while, however, you hear a story where you wonder to yourself how the domestic staff put up with the absurd tasks given by their bosses. Here is one of those stories:

Foreign diplomats are allowed to import a car into Indonesia tax-free. When their assignment is finished, they are allowed to bring it back to their home country without paying the substantial luxury tax. One of the requirements to return a vehicle to the Netherlands free of tax is that it must be used with at least 10,000 kilometers.

A Dutch guy working at the Netherlands embassy tried to do just that. He began the process of buying a car a year or so after his arrival, and after all the paperwork was processed he finally received his new tax-free car. Unfortunately, he only took delivery of his car a few months before his assignment was finished. Even worse, he learned about the 10,000 kilometer regulation when he was almost ready to go back, and he was 7,000 kilometers short! So in his final weeks in Indonesia his told his driver to hit the toll road and drive from Jakarta to Bogor and back – five to six times each day. And because the steering wheel of this car was on the left side and the toll window was on the right, this guy told the gardener to join the driver in the car to help pay the tolls.

When I heard this story, I couldn't help but wonder what was going through the minds of the driver and the gardener as they drove the 50 kilometer toll road to Bogor and back – an incredible 70 times. Maybe they thought it was some kind of punishment for something. Or perhaps they just didn't care and just drove in silence the entire time. Well, whatever they were thinking, I am sure it ended with two words: BULE GILA!

happy ending

It seems time goes by quickly in Indonesia. I have come up with a plan to safeguard my last days in Indonesia. A retirement home for expats, somewhere between Bogor and Sukabumi on the cool slopes of Mount Salak. Imagine: you are 60+ and are served every day with friendly smiles. The day starts with a bath in a hot water spring, followed by an English breakfast and a morning walk through the rice paddies or tea gardens. Then you can choose between playing golf at one the many courses around the Bogor area or join the group that goes to one of the – by that time – 100+ shopping malls. The golfers will have a massage at the course or – more convenient – use the 24-hour service in the retirement home. In the afternoon there is a pool competition between the European, American and Asian residents. If you don't like pool you can watch Grease or a replay of the 1974 World Cup. The satellite internet connection provides free video chatting with the family back home. As most of the retired expats have still a wide network of connections, it is easy for them to find sources for charity projects they can work on. Others just work on their hobbies like brewing beer. Or teach English in the *kampung*.

A BuGils branch is open 24 hours and has the same staff as it did when it first started. The management has arranged discounts for every bar, on every golf course and with every airline in the country. It is a great idea. It will be cheaper than a retirement home in Europe, where the family will visit you once a week on a Sunday morning without actually enjoying it. Here, if you feel lonely, you can hire visitors. Visitors for rent. Wives on contract. Fashion shows for the ladies. Daily spa treatments. The management can arrange it all! And the name of this retirement home? HAPPY ENDING! Retire With A Smile.

you know you've been in jakarta too long if...

The following is the most hilarious part of the book, probably because I didn't write it myself. I shamelessly copied it from Malcom's excellent website www.jakartablokm.com. If anyone has additions to this list email me at bartele@bugils.com.

You know you've been in Jakarta too long if...
   * The footprints on the toilet seat are your own.

   * You no longer wait in line, but immediately go to the head of the queue.

   * You loiter at the bottom of an escalator to plan your day.

   * You habitually punch all the buttons as you exit the lift.

   * It has become exciting to see if you can get into the lift before others can get out.

   * You're willing to pay to use a toilet you wouldn't go to within a kilometer of at home.

   * It is no longer surprising that the only decision made at a meeting is the time and venue of the next meeting.

   * You rank the decision-making abilities of your staff by how long it takes them to reply "up to you mister".

   * You no longer wonder how someone making US$200 per month can drive a Mercedes.

* You accept the fact that you have to queue to get your number for the next queue.

* You have considered buying a motorcycle for the next family car.

* You accept without question the mechanic's analysis that your car is "broken", and that it will cost you a lot of money to get it fixed.

* You find it saves time to stand and retrieve your cabin baggage while the plane is still on final approach.

* You think the Proton and Kijang are stylish and well-built cars.

* You walk to the pub with your arm around your mate.

* You walk into a five-star hotel lobby unshaven and in jogging shorts, ratty t-shirt and flip-flops, without worrying what the management might think.

* You answer the telephone with "Hello" more than two times.

* You are quite content to repeat your order six times in a restaurant that only has four items on the menu.

* A T-bone steak and rice sounds just fine.

* You believe everything you read in the local newspaper.

* You habitually ignore traffic signals, stop signs and copy-watch peddlers.

* When listening to the pilot prove he can't speak English, you no longer wonder how he can understand the air traffic controllers.

* You regard it as part of an adventure when the waiter exactly repeats your order, and then the cook makes something completely different.

* You're not surprised when three men with a ladder show up to change a light bulb.

* You think it is normal to wait six days to get your laundry back or pay 50% surcharge for same day service.

* Taxi drivers understand you.

* You own a rice cooker.

* You consider that 5 kbps is a pretty good download speed.

* Due to selective memory you honestly believe you could return to the Western world.

* You can shake your hands almost perfectly dry before wiping them on your pants.

* You look at a pin-up photo of Demi Moore and think that she is rather unattractive.

* When crossing a busy street you believe that a limp wrist motion with your right arm creates a force field that repels oncoming traffic.

* Suitable family entertainment for a Friday night is to dress the whole family in dark clothing and dash back and forth across Jalan Sudirman and other busy streets.

* You keep a supply of plain brown envelopes in your desk drawer.

* You understand all of the above references!

also from
EQUINOX PUBLISHING